CW00469921

Meals Without Meat

Marion Raymond

BAY BOOKS, LONDON & SYDNEY

About the author

Marion Raymond, now Cooking Editor for Bay Books, has been interested in food since childhood. She settled in Australia twenty years ago after living for many years in Europe and Africa. Her career as a journalist led to an increasing involvement in cooking, and she has been practising both professions for most of her life.

In Australia, Marion Raymond is probably best known for her column in *The Bulletin* in which, for some five years, she extolled the delights of good food prepared in the simplest manner.

1979 published by Bay Books
Pty Ltd
157-167 Bayswater Road,
Rushcutters Bay
NSW 2011 Australia
© 1979 Bay Books
National Library of Australia
Card Number and ISBN
0 85835 379 2
All the recipes in this book are in
metric measure; temperatures are
given in degrees centigrade.

Contents

Introduction

At last people have begun to realise that good health is not based on eating large quantities of meat! And the present day price of meat is not the only reason. Although this book is not written for vegetarians, many of the recipes will prove useful for those of you who are.

When planning a meal which has no substantial main course such as a chicken or a joint, care must be taken to create a varied menu. Forget the standard two or three course menu. A meatless menu must feature several complementary courses of equal importance. A well balanced meal will ensure pleasure as well as good health.

One of the things that encouraged me to compile this book was a meal a friend of mine had one night. She was taken to a vegetarian dinner. When I asked her how it was she said it was nice but rather boring. She had three courses and every one of them consisted of the same vegetables only slightly differently prepared. What she really meant to say was that both she and her appetite were bored!

Appetite is kindled by appearance, and a contrast of flavours is just as important as the different values of the food you eat. Concentrate on attractive presentation of food because the way it looks plays a large part in the success of any meal.

Think of the first course of your meal as an overture, a promise of what is to come. Keep it small but interesting whether it is soup, a small portion of pasta, or even a soufflé. Follow it up with a complete contrast of texture as well as flavour. Then repeat the process with the next dish.

If economy is one of your aims when not serving meat, remember to plan your meals around seasonal foods. Freeze or bottle food when it's plentiful. Before herbs come to the season's end chop and freeze them in ice cubes for easy storage in plastic bags; herbs are invaluable for bringing out the best flavour of any meal. My Italian greengrocer is always amused when I tell him to remind me when supplies of basil are becoming scarce. I chop mine finely, prepare a good stock to pour over it, and then freeze it in cubes. He chops his with a little garlic and stores it in jars covered in olive oil. Our customs are different but we both have fresh basil to last through the winter! When parsley is at its best I trim the stalks and place the leaves in the bowl of my food processor. Using the metal blade I give it a short burst and then roll up the parsley in greaseproof paper and place it in the freezer. I cut off what I need and leave the remainder in the freezer.

The recipes given in this book come from a number of different countries and, as I think you undoubtedly have a spirit of adventure, I hope you will enjoy reading this book and making that little extra effort in planning a successful meal without meat.

Marion Raymond

APPETISERS AND STARTERS

Sometimes I think that planning a good menu is rather like writing a good book. The beginning should attract enough attention to make you want to continue; the middle should hold your attention; and the ending should be memorable.

When entertaining, I am one of those people who believe nuts and chips should be strictly reserved for drinks which are not going to be followed with a meal. I like to see my guests reach the table willing and able to eat all that is going to be placed in front of them. Tidbits, in my opinion, take the edge off one's appetite.

The recipes in this section are intended to whet the appetite. You may like to choose something for a drinks party or you might decide to serve one of the recipes as a first course. After all, there is no rule which stipulates that all good meals must start with soup.

When planning your meal just bear in mind that it is always best to leave the table wishing that there was just a little more to eat, rather than regretting having eaten too much.

Avocado Mousse

Serves 4

¼ cup water
1 tbls gelatine
2 avocados, mashed
2 tbls lemon juice
½ tsp salt
3 tbls Worcestershire sauce
1 cup cream
½ cup mayonnaise

Dissolve gelatine and water over simmering water. Blend avocado with lemon juice, salt and Worcestershire sauce. Whip cream until almost stiff, fold in mayonnaise. Add melted gelatine to cream, then fold in avocado mixture. Cover and allow to set in refrigerator. Serve on a crisp lettuce leaf and decorate with very thin slices of lemon. For a special occasion decorate mousse with 1 tsp of black caviar or lumpfish.

Caviar Mousse

Serves 4

1 tbls gelatine dissolved in
4 tbls water
1 cup cream
2 tbls horseradish
¼ tsp salt
2 small jars pink caviar,
or lumpfish
2 hard boiled eggs, quartered
4 very thin slices lemon

Dissolve gelatine over simmering water. Whip cream, fold in horseradish, salt and cooled gelatine. Reserve a little caviar for decoration and fold in remainder to cream mixture, taking care not to break globules. Cover and allow to set in small individual soufflé dishes. Serve turned out on a slice of toast, decorate with reserved caviar, egg and lemon slices.

Stuffed Tomatoes with Anchovies

Serves 6

6 large tomatoes
2 small tins anchovy fillets
½ cup fresh breadcrumbs
½ teaspoon oregano
grated cheese

Slice tops off tomatoes and scoop pulp into a small bowl. Mash anchovies in their oil and mix with breadcrumbs. Soften with some of the scooped out pulp which has been strained of seeds. Fill tomatoes. Sprinkle with grated cheese and place in a moderate oven for 20 minutes.

Eggplant Starter

Serves 6

3 medium eggplants
salt
3-4 tbls flour
1 egg, beaten
½ cup breadcrumbs
grated rind of 1 lemon
mixture of butter and oil
for frying

Cut eggplants into thick slices and cover with salt. Allow to rest for 15 minutes. Wash salt off and dry with kitchen paper. Lightly dust with flour. Dip into beaten egg and coat with crumbs which have been mixed with lemon rind. Fry until golden on both sides. Drain on kitchen paper and keep warm in low oven. To serve, top with following suggestions:

☐ grilled mushroom caps filled with finely chopped parsley and a squeeze of garlic
☐ puréed spinach sweetened with a little cream and a pinch of nutmeg
☐ bacon sippets mixed with bread croûtons lightly fried in bacon fat
☐ tomato wedges grilled and dusted with oregano.

Guacamole

For this versatile Mexican dish it is good to look for over-ripe avocados. These can often be purchased cheaply and the mixture can be made and frozen for later use. Guacamole can be served as a starter on a lettuce leaf, as a filling for omelettes or tacos, a party dip to be eaten with taco chips, and is delicious diluted and used as a salad dressing.

2 ripe avocados
juice of 1 lemon or lime
½ tsp salt
1 large onion, grated
1 clove garlic, crushed
1 tsp curry powder
pinch cayenne
dash Tabasco sauce (optional)

Mash avocado with a fork. Work in lemon juice and salt. Mix onion with garlic, add to avocado with remaining ingredients. Cover with plastic wrap and chill to serve. If to be used for a salad dressing, omit curry, and blend in a little olive oil to dilute the mixture. Mayonnaise instead of oil may also be used if it is intended as a dressing.

Stuffed Capsicums, Chinese Style

Serves 8

4 green capsicums
6 hard boiled eggs, chopped
3 tsp soy sauce
¼ tsp salt
½ tsp Szechwan peppers, ground
½ tsp finely chopped green ginger
6 water chestnuts, halved
4 shallots, finely chopped
2 tsp sesame oil

Halve capsicums lengthwise, remove seeds. Combine eggs, soy sauce, salt, ginger, peppers, water chestnuts and shallots. Fill into halved capsicums and place on a rack in a large fry pan. Pour boiling water into pan below level of rack, cover with a lid and steam over moderate heat for 20 minutes. Sprinkle with sesame oil and serve hot.

Pease Puddings with Fresh Tomato Sauce

Serves 6-8

3 tbls butter
3 tbls flour
½ cup milk, warmed slightly
3 cups shelled peas
1 cup water
1 tsp salt
1 tbls chopped mint
2 tsp gelatine
2 tbls dry sherry
½ cup chicken stock
1 cup cream, whipped
watercress for decoration
1 quantity fresh tomato sauce
(recipe p. 94)

Prepare velouté sauce by melting butter and stirring in flour to make a roux. Remove from heat, stir in milk, return to heat to thicken and cook flour. Set aside. Cook peas in water with salt and mint for 6 minutes. Drain and purée in blender or food processor, add roux and chicken stock. Melt gelatine in sherry over hot water, add to purée and cool. Whip cream, add to cooled purée and pour into individual soufflé dishes. Chill in refrigerator to set and serve decorated with watercress sprigs and fresh tomato sauce.

Prawn Toasts

Serves 4

8 slices French bread
butter
1 clove garlic, crushed
250 g prawns, cooked and peeled
lemon juice
1 tbls parsley, finely chopped
salt and freshly ground pepper

Butter bread on both sides and fry until golden. Crush garlic, mash with prawns and lemon juice. Mix in parsley and season to taste. Spread on fried bread and brown quickly under griller to serve.

Oyster Patties

Serves 6

12 thin slices of wholemeal bread
4 spinach leaves, trimmed of
stalks
1 wine glass of light curry sauce
24 oysters, fresh or bottled and
drained

Remove crusts and cut bread into triangles. Place 2 triangles into each of 6 oiled patty tins and press into shape. Allow to brown lightly in a moderate oven. Meanwhile, blanch spinach leaves briefly in boiling salt water and drain. Line patty shells with spinach leaves. Place 4 oysters into each shell, top with a little warm curry sauce and serve as appetisers.

Smoked Oysters in Mushrooms

Serves 4

8 medium sized field mushrooms
1 tin smoked oysters
2 tbls lemon juice
2 tbls fresh breadcrumbs
1 tbls parsley, finely chopped

Peel and stalk mushrooms, place on foil in griller pan. Mash oysters and their oil with lemon juice, breadcrumbs and parsley. Fill into mushroom caps and place under hot griller to cook mushrooms. Serve immediately.

Deep Fried Mushrooms

Serves 6

24 small mushrooms
1 egg, beaten
1 cup dry breadcrumbs
1 tbls parsley, finely chopped
salt and freshly ground pepper
1 clove garlic

Wipe mushrooms with a damp cloth. Dip into egg. Mix breadcrumbs with parsley, salt and pepper. Coat mushrooms with mixture. Place garlic clove into hot oil and deep fry mushrooms. Drain on kitchen paper and serve 4 per person with a spoonful of mayonnaise and a quartered lemon.

Alternative: mix breadcrumbs with 2 tbls Parmesan cheese and a little grated lemon peel.

Egg Toadstools

Serves 6

6 hard boiled eggs, peeled
1 tbls anchovy paste
1 tbls cream
1 whitloof (Belgian endive),
shredded
1 tbls lemon juice
salt and freshly ground pepper
6 pickled mushroom caps
(recipe p.15)

Cut tops off eggs and scoop out yolks carefully. Mash with anchovy paste and cream. Fill back into eggs. Prepare whitloof with lemon juice, salt and pepper. Spoon onto small plates. Stand eggs up in the middle of plates (use a little more anchovy paste to secure eggs if necessary). Place mushroom cap on top of egg.

Greek Dolmades

Serves 6-8

40 vine leaves
1 cup brown rice
½ cup olive oil
¼ cup pine nuts
1 cup chopped shallots
1 tbls chopped parsley
1 tbls chopped fresh herbs
¼ cup currants soaked in juice of
2 lemons
1 cup tomato purée
1 cup stock to cover vine leaves

Blanch leaves briefly in boiling water and dry. Cook rice then drain but do not rinse. Heat 2 tbls oil in saucepan and sauté shallots. Add rice, pine nuts, parsley, herbs and drained currants. Reserve lemon juice. Season to taste with salt and pepper. Cook 5 minutes and cool. Fill vine leaves with mixture, fold and roll. Place into large shallow casserole lined with remaining leaves. Combine lemon juice with tomato purée, stock and remaining olive oil, pour over dolmades. Weight them with a heavy lid and simmer 40 minutes. Serve cold or hot. If serving them hot, thicken sauce with a little cornflour first blended with a little water.

Chinese Lotus Flowers

Makes 18

500 g green prawns
10 water chestnuts
4 spring onions
½ tsp freshly grated ginger
½ tsp salt
1 tbls dry sherry
1 egg white
1 tsp cornflour
oil for deep frying

Shell, vein and chop prawns. Chop water chestnuts and spring onions. Add prawns, ginger, salt and sherry. Whisk egg white until stiff, add to prawn mixture. Sprinkle with cornflour and shape into small balls. Heat oil; when hot, deep fry until golden. Drain and serve immediately.

Pickled Eggs

Serve these as a starter with a mixed salad, or keep them handy as a snack to accompany a drink. I learnt this recipe in Canada and found it very good. The eggs will keep for at least a month at room temperature.

12 hard-boiled eggs, shelled
2 cups white wine vinegar
½ cup water
2 tsp salt
12 whole cloves
2 pieces root ginger, peeled
1 teaspoon whole black pepper
1 bay leaf

Place eggs into a large sterilised pickling jar. Combine vinegar, water and all remaining ingredients in a saucepan and bring to the boil. Chill and strain. Pour over eggs to cover, adding more vinegar if necessary. Cover jars and allow to stand at least 2 days before using.

Pickled Mushrooms

250 g small mushrooms (if not
particularly small, remove stalks)
1 bouquet garni
1 clove garlic, peeled
1½ cups white wine vinegar
1 tsp salt
6 peppercorns

Clean mushrooms with a damp cloth. Heat vinegar with bouquet garni. Place mushrooms into sterilised glass jar. Add garlic, salt and peppercorns. Remove bouquet garni and pour vinegar over mushrooms to cover. Cool, then seal jar and allow to rest at least 2 days before using. Serve several on a lettuce leaf as a starter, or serve as accompaniment to a main course.

SOUPS

Soups are splendid and versatile. They can be the prelude to a feast or a meal on their own. There was a time when no self-respecting cook would start a meal without one, and many hours were devoted to its preparation. The happy accident of former years was that while vegetables were over-cooked in too much water, which destroyed their vitamins and minerals, the water in which they were cooked was reserved for the stock pot. So, although the vegetables lost all their goodness, the soup replenished all that was lost!

Today the stock pot does not enjoy much popularity and more's the pity: it doesn't take long to make, nor is it complicated. The ingredients don't have to be measured, but it is essential to make a well balanced stock. Too many tomatoes, turnips or celery will overpower the flavour; too many carrots will turn it brown. A boiled chicken or a bone will produce a stock which will gel, and from which you can make a good cold consommé; a cube will not do this. Add a little wine to your stock, it will enhance the flavour and improve its keeping qualities.

Don't ignore soups in the summer. If your palate doesn't fancy a hot one, serve a chilled variety. If using cream in a soup sounds like too many calories, replace the cream with low-fat sour cream, or even yoghurt. Above all, make your soup bowl look appealing. Decorate it with something splendid: a single prawn, a twist of lemon dipped in finely chopped parsley, a slice of avocado, a sprig of watercress.

Cold Orange Consommé

Chilled Cherry Soup

Serves 6

½ k dark cherries
4 cups water
125 g sugar
pinch salt
rind of 1 lemon, thinly pared
small stick cinnamon
2 tsp flour
1 egg yolk
1 cup sour cream
1 cup dry red wine

Stone cherries and slowly bring to the boil with water, sugar, salt, lemon peel and cinnamon. Lower heat immediately and simmer until tender. Mix flour in a bowl with egg yolk and half sour cream. Blend in 1 spoonful of warm soup then pour into simmering soup, stirring constantly. When thickened stir in wine and remaining sour cream. Allow to simmer 10 minutes. Take out lemon peel and cinnamon, chill before serving.

Cold Orange Consommé

Serves 6

5 cups cold chicken stock
15 g gelatine
2 egg whites, whisked
2½ cups fresh orange juice, strained
small cinnamon stick
watercress sprigs for decoration
1 unpeeled orange, very thinly sliced, for decoration

Stock cubes will not be suitable for this soup. Either use reserved strained stock from a boiled chicken or make stock from a chicken wing. Strain and bring stock to the boil. Whisk egg whites into boiling stock. When stock foams and rises, stir in gelatine. Remove from heat and allow to rest 5 minutes. Strain through damp muslin or teacloth. Stir in orange juice and allow to rest, undisturbed, until cool. Refrigerate overnight. Serve in chilled soup bowls garnished with sprig of watercress and thin slice of orange.

Gazpacho

Serves 8

This Spanish cold vegetable soup comes in many versions. Some are so basic that they are literally made with garlic, breadcrumbs, oil vinegar and water. This one is rather fancy but, if you own a blender or food processor, it is made in minutes.

6 cloves garlic
1 tbls salt
1 tbls sugar
2 tbls paprika
6 tbls olive oil
2 tbls wine vinegar
pinch cayenne
1 k ripe tomatoes, peeled
4 cups chicken stock (can be made with stock cubes)
1 cucumber
24 shallots
1-2 green capsicums

Place first 7 ingredients into blender. When thick, add tomatoes. If using processor you may have to make this in 2 batches, depending on size of machine. Pour into a large bowl and add cooled stock. Peel cucumber and dice. Add to bowl, cover with plastic film and place into refrigerator to chill. Chop shallots and capsicum, place into individual bowls and sprinkle over soup when chilled. Pour soup over ice cubes to serve.

Instant Chilled Tomato and Avocado Soup

Serves 6

½ k ripe tomatoes, peeled and
puréed in blender
1 onion
1 cucumber
1 avocado
½ tsp oregano
3 tbls oil
2 tbls wine vinegar
pinch sugar
salt and pepper to taste

Purée tomatoes. Chop cucumber, onion, and blend with avocado. Add oregano, oil and vinegar. Mix with tomato juice and pour over ice cubes placed in individual soup bowls. Decorate with thin slice of cucumber or avocado.

Italian Minestrone

Serves 6

1 tbls oil
1 small slice smoked pork, diced
(optional)
1 clove garlic crushed
1 medium onion, sliced
1 tbls parsley, finely chopped
1 tbls fresh basil or oregano,
finely chopped
1 tsp salt and freshly ground
pepper
1 tbls tomato paste mixed with
½ cup water
3 stalks celery, chopped
3 carrots, sliced
2 potatoes, sliced
1 cup cooked dried peas
¼ head cabbage, shredded
3 zucchini, sliced
1 cup peas
6 cups water
1 cup elbow macaroni
grated Parmesan cheese

In a large soup pot heat oil, add pork, garlic, onion, parsley, basil, salt and pepper. Allow onion to colour slightly, then stir in blended tomato paste. Cook 5 minutes. Add vegetables and water, simmer for 35 minutes. Add macaroni and cook 8 minutes. Serve sprinkled with grated Parmesan cheese.

Chestnut Soup

Serves 6

50 g chestnuts
1½ litre chicken stock
(cubes may be used)
1 medium onion, sliced
1 leek, white part only,
sliced
1 carrot, sliced
3 sticks celery, chopped
½ tsp salt
pinch sugar
dash cayenne
1 cup cream
2 tbls dry sherry
fried bread croûtons, optional

— combine

Peel chestnuts and cook them in the combined stock until tender. With a slotted spoon remove and reserve 6 whole chestnuts. Process remainder with stock in a blender or food processor. Return to pan and reheat. Stir in cream and sherry but do not allow to boil. Pour into soup bowls, decorate with reserved chestnuts and pass croûtons separately.

Lentil Soup

Serves 4-6

250 g brown lentils
1 onion, finely chopped
1 clove garlic, crushed
2 tbls parsley, finely chopped
2 tbls oil
2 large tomatoes, skinned and
seeded
salt and pepper
2 tbls wine vinegar (optional)

Soak lentils in water for at least 1 hour. Rinse, cover with fresh salted water, bring to the boil and simmer 1 hour. Lightly fry onion, garlic and parsley. Add tomatoes and stir fry 5 minutes. Add to lentils and reheat before serving. Vinegar gives a pleasant sharp taste to this nutritious soup.

Cheese Soup

Serves 6

6 tbls butter
5 tbls flour
4 cups warm milk
1 cup cream
250 g Gouda cheese, grated
125 g smoked cheese, grated
2 tbls Worcestershire sauce
1 tsp paprika
dash of Tabasco sauce

Melt butter in heavy saucepan and stir in flour to make a roux, remove from heat and stir in warmed milk. Return to heat and allow flour to cook through. Stir constantly until perfectly smooth. Gradually add both cheeses and continue to stir until cheese has melted. Add cream and heat through but do not allow to boil. Just before serving add remaining ingredients and season to taste.

Serving suggestions:

☐ decorate soup with sippets of bread fried in butter and garlic
☐ deep fry ice cold parsley sprigs quickly and float on soup
☐ brown some sesame seeds in the oven and sprinkle on soup

Spicy Chicken and Avocado Soup

Serves 6

6 cups chicken stock (stock cubes can be used)
1 chicken breast
2 onions, thinly sliced
½ tsp coriander
½ tsp oregano
1 tsp curry powder
½ tsp salt and freshly ground pepper
1 large avocado

Place chicken breast in stock with onions and the next 5 ingredients. Bring to the boil, then simmer for 20 minutes. Remove chicken, cool, strain stock and discard onion. Remove skin from chicken and slice meat into julienne strips. Just before soup is required, heat through with chicken strips. Peel avocado and slice thinly. Place slices into individual soup bowls and pour soup over. Slices will float to the top.

Cream of Avocado Soup

Serves 6

1 onion, thinly sliced
1 stalk celery, chopped
2 tbls butter
2 tbls flour
2 chicken stock cubes dissolved in 2 cups hot water
1 tbls lemon juice
1 tbls horseradish
1 clove garlic, crushed
1 tsp curry powder
salt and freshly ground pepper
sprinkle of tarragon and allspice
1 avocado
1 cup milk
1 cup cream
bacon sippets, optional decoration

Sauté onion and celery in butter until tender. Stir in flour. Make a roux, stir in stock and cook until smooth. Add lemon juice, horseradish, garlic, curry powder and salt. Simmer for 5 minutes. Dust lightly with pepper, tarragon and allspice. Peel avocado, mash with a fork, stir a little soup into avocado then add to soup and blend. Add milk, cream, and warm through but do not boil. Serve garnished with fried and crumbled bacon sippets, if desired.

Chinese Green Soup

Serves 4-6

1 tbls peanut oil
½ tsp grated fresh ginger
1 clove garlic, crushed
5 cups hot chicken stock (cubes may be used)
1 cup boiled rice
750 g Chinese cabbage, finely shredded
6 spring onions, finely chopped
1 tbls dry sherry
½ tsp sesame oil

Heat oil and stir fry ginger and garlic 1 minute. Add hot stock and boiled rice. Simmer 15 minutes. Add cabbage and spring onions, simmer 5 minutes. When vegetables are cooked, stir in sherry and sesame oil.

Creole Schnapper Soup

Serves 6

6 fillets red schnapper
reserved fish heads
few small pieces of non-oily fish
3 medium onions, sliced
2 bay leaves
1 bouquet garni
salt and freshly ground pepper
2 cloves garlic, chopped
few sprigs parsley
½ tsp allspice
olive oil
6 tomatoes, skinned and chopped
1 lemon, very thinly sliced
1 cup dry white wine
1 tbls curry powder
6 pieces fried bread

Place fish heads and small pieces of fish into a large saucepan with 5 cups water, 1 onion, bay leaves, bouquet garni and salt and pepper. Boil and allow to reduce. Remove head, bouquet garni, and strain. Set aside. Pound or blend garlic with parsley and allspice and rub into fish fillets. Heat 2 tbls oil in a wide pan, add remaining onion, top with fish fillets. Cover and simmer 10 minutes, turning fish once. Remove and keep warm. To pan add tomatoes and stir 5 minutes. Add lemon slices, strained stock, wine and curry powder. Simmer 5 minutes. Add fish to heat through. Meanwhile fry bread, place into soup bowls, cover each with a fish fillet and pour hot soup over.

CREPES

Once upon a time crêpes were reserved for the end of a meal. Now they have been elevated and are often served as a starter or even a meal on their own. To be at their best, crêpes must be thin and moist, not heavy or overcooked. Always prepare the mixture and then allow it to rest in the refrigerator for at least 2 hours before using it.

Your crêpe pan should be one that is reserved strictly for crêpes and omelettes. Never use a metal implement in the pan as any scratches will later cause sticking. Always clean the pan only with a mild detergent and a sponge.

Crêpes can be made in advance and will even keep several days when frozen: stack them between waxed paper and then place them in a freezer bag. In this way you can use them as required. In an emergency you can make an almost instant snack by filling them with left-overs blended into a light sauce.

When expecting a crowd, consider serving a variety of filled crêpes. Bring the meal to a close with a selection of salads and a cheese board and there is little to distract you from enjoying your party as all the preparations have been made in advance.

There are two ways to prepare for such an event. Either make and fill the crêpes, then roll and place them side by side into a shallow rectangular baking dish. Pour over a suitable sauce, such as a light tomato, cheese or simple béchamel sauce, cover the dish with foil and heat it through in a moderate oven when necessary. The other way is to prepare a large quantity of crêpes and a selection of fillings to be served hot from fondue dishes. Allow your guests to re-heat their crêpes in a pan over a small spirit-lamp and then select their filling. You'll be surprised to see how much fun your guests will have.

Crêpe Batter

Makes 16 crêpes

250 g plain flour, sifted
3 eggs
440 ml mixture of half milk
and water
3 tbls melted butter

If you own a blender or food processor place the first 2 ingredients into the bowl and blend 1-2 seconds. While the motor is running add the liquids and blend until smooth. When making the batter by hand, place flour into a bowl. Make a well in the middle and add eggs, blend, then add liquids and form a smooth batter with a rotary beater.

Preparation

Melt a little butter in your crêpe pan over medium heat. Once frothing, pour 2 tablespoons of batter, sufficient to barely cover the base of your pan and swirl around. As air bubbles rise, shake the pan to free the crêpe, then toss or turn over quickly with a spatula and cook for a few seconds to firm. Each crêpe should take scarcely 1 minute to cook. Crêpes can be kept warm in a low oven if to be used immediately. If to be stored, stack between waxed paper. When required, fill crêpes as desired and re-heat crêpes in a low oven.

Suggestions for Crêpe Fillings

Prepare ½ litre of tomato sauce (recipe p. 94). Sauté 10 chopped shallots and 1 clove crushed garlic in a small knob of butter for 1 minute. Add 125 g scallops cut in half. Sauté 3 minutes. Add 125 g cooked chopped prawns. Sauté 3 minutes. Add tomato sauce, heat through and blend. Fill crêpes and roll.

Prepare ½ litre hollandaise sauce. Steam ¼ k broccoli flowers. Mash with a fork and add to sauce. Blend in 1 tbls capers and fill crêpes with this mixture.

Prepare ½ litre béchamel sauce (recipe p. 93). Steam 250 g fillet of fish. Flake into béchamel. Add 1 tbls brandy and 1 tbls finely chopped dill. Fill into crêpes and roll.

Peel, seed and dice 1 cucumber. Sauté in 1 tbls butter with 1 tbls minced onion for 10 minutes until excess moisture evaporates. Set aside. Melt 1 tbls butter, stir in 1 tbls flour and make a roux with ½ cup milk. When thickened and cooked, season to taste. Mash 1 small avocado with 1 tsp grated lemon rind and 2 tbls lemon juice. Add cucumber and onion, and mash. Heat through before filling crêpes but do not allow to boil.

Prepare ½ litre of béchamel sauce. Stir in 3 tbls creamed spinach and 1 tbls lemon juice. Lightly sauté 3 tbls pine nuts in small knob of butter to colour, strain butter off and add to sauce mixture. Fill crêpes and roll.

Party Crêpes with Mushroom sauce

Prepare ½ litre mushroom sauce (recipe p. 93). Lightly sauté 10 chopped spring onions. Add contents of small tin of drained tuna and fork through. Add 3 tbls tinned peas and heat through. Add mushroom sauce, adjust seasoning and add 1 tsp grated lemon rind. Fill into crêpes and roll.

Crêpe Soufflé
Makes 16 crêpes

½ litre of crêpe batter
375 ml béchamel sauce
4 eggs, separated
50 g Gruyère cheese, diced

Preheat oven to 200°C and prepare crêpes as directed, stacking in a flat pile on a plate. Prepare béchamel sauce with egg yolks, add diced cheese. Whisk egg whites until stiff, then fold gently into béchamel sauce. Fill each crêpe with some of the soufflé mixture and fold over to enclose. Place crêpes on a greased ovenproof dish and bake for 12 minutes until filling is cooked through.

Italian Crêpes

Prepare crêpes as directed. Chop ½ cup of ham and a similar quantity of Mozzarella cheese. Mix well with 1 tbls finely chopped parsley, fill crêpes and roll. Place side by side in a shallow baking dish and almost cover them with a good chicken stock. Heat through in a moderate oven.

Parmesan Crêpes

Prepare batter for crêpes as directed. After the addition of the melted butter, add 4 tbls of finely grated Parmesan cheese and a pinch of salt. Beat well and allow batter to rest for 2 hours before using. Beat again before using.

Serving suggestions:
☐ fill crêpes with a little ricotta cheese first blended with a little cream and spiced with paprika
☐ blend some puréed spinach into cream cheese and add a few chopped walnuts, then fill and roll crêpes
☐ wrap crêpes around a few spears of warm asparagus and sprinkle with grated Parmesan cheese
☐ wrap crêpes around warm spears of heart of palm
☐ lie crêpe flat on a plate, pour over a thick mushroom sauce, top with another crêpe; repeat several times and construct a crêpe cake, then cut into wedges to serve
☐ fill crêpes with warm ratatouille (recipe p. 64) and roll to serve

Swiss Crêpes

Prepare batter as directed. Cook and fold crêpes in half. When all crêpes are cooked and folded place a thick slice of Mozzarella cheese on each quarter of crêpe. Fold to enclose. Seal edges with a little beaten egg white. Heat oil for deep frying and fry each crêpe in deep fat until light gold. Drain on kitchen paper. Keep warm in oven until ready to serve. One or two make an excellent entrée, or they can be served with a salad for a light luncheon. A slice of ham the same size as the cheese can also be inserted.

Parmesan Crêpes with Asparagus Spears

SALADS

After numerous visits to America I am convinced that in that country one will find the best salads served anywhere in the world. This stands to reason when one considers that country's population. There are salads from all over the world, hot and cold, and anything can be turned into a taste experience. All American restaurants feature a chef's salad on their menu, as well as a long list of well-liked traditional salads, and the chef's salad is usually the speciality of the house . . . it should never be missed. It is here that the chef, like an artist, lets you share his special talent.

One should eat salads not because they are good for one, but because they are a joy to eat and delicious to remember. A good salad can be served purely as a taste tempter for what is to follow. A small salad can accompany a meal, a larger one can be the main course, and a crisp astringent one can even be the finale to a meal.

The best ingredients are, without a doubt, home grown: young and tender. If this is not possible then choose the ingredients with a critical eye. Look for variety in lettuce. Avoid limp or wilted greens and never, ever buy them wrapped in plastic. Don't keep greens in the refrigerator longer than absolutely necessary. Wash leaves in cold water and shake the water off, preferably in a lettuce basket so that the lettuce is not bruised. Wet leaves result in a soggy salad. Tear leaves apart and never cut them.

One either loves garlic and onions or detests them. Settle for a hint of flavour rather than too much. A clove of garlic can be used to rub around a salad bowl and then discarded. Or crush a clove with a little salt and use the resultant juice. Take it easy with the onions unless you really love them.

Fresh herbs can make any salad something special, but use them with discretion: too many varieties used at the same time can drown the flavour of all of them.

Salad dressings can be made in advance and stored in a bottle — but don't keep them too long! Purists prefer to coat lettuce with oil, and only when every leaf is lightly coated and gleaming do they add the remaining ingredients. Use only the very best oils and be sparing with vinegar. Wine vinegars or plain lemon juice are best.

Savoury Rock Melon Salad

Savoury Rock Melon Salad

Serves 6

3 rock melons, halved and
scooped
4 tbls lemon juice
½ cup mayonnaise
¼ cup sour cream
1 tbls lemon rind, grated
1 tbls basil, finely chopped
2 cups white chicken, cubed
1 tsp ground ginger
1 tsp salt
freshly ground white pepper
1 cup green grapes, halved and
seeded
1 red capsicum, seeded and diced
1 cup celery, threaded and sliced
toasted almond slivers

Cut rock melons and scoop out pips. Sprinkle with a little lemon juice. Mix mayonnaise with sour cream, add lemon rind and remaining lemon juice. Dust chicken with ginger, salt and pepper, fold into mayonnaise. Add grapes, capsicum and celery. Fill into melons and sprinkle with toasted almonds to serve.

Grape Salad

Serves 6

1 Cos lettuce
3 cups chilled grapes, green and
black
1 medium cucumber, thinly sliced
¼ cup olive oil
lemon juice
salt and freshly ground pepper
2 tbls chopped shallots

Prepare individual salad bowls by lining with torn lettuce leaves. Top with mixture of grapes. Scatter cucumber over grapes. Mix with olive oil with lemon juice and seasoning in a glass jar, cover and shake, pour over salad and sprinkle with shallots.

Celery and Mushroom Salad

Serves 6-8

1 head young celery
250 g mushrooms
1 tbls finely chopped basil
6 tbls oil
2 tbls wine vinegar
salt and freshly ground pepper
60 g blue cheese

Trim and wash celery well. Slice thinly and dry thoroughly with tea towel. Wipe mushrooms with damp cloth and slice thinly, discarding stalks. Place both into salad bowl and dust with basil. Sprinkle with oil, toss well, sprinkle with vinegar and toss again. Season to taste and crumble blue cheese over to serve.

Snake Bean Salad

Spinach and Mushroom Salad

Serves 4-6

1 bunch very young spinach
(sometimes called English
spinach)
125 g button mushrooms, thinly
sliced, stalks removed
2-3 tbls best olive oil
juice of half a lemon
½ tsp salt and freshly ground
black pepper
1 tsp finely chopped fresh basil
or
1 tbls finely chopped chives

Wash and dry spinach well. Remove stalks and tear into bite-sized pieces. Slice mushrooms thinly. Place spinach into salad bowl, sprinkle with oil and toss lightly. Add mushrooms and sprinkle with lemon juice. Dust with black pepper and herbs. Toss lightly and serve.

Alternative: place prepared spinach into salad bowl, fry two chopped rashers of bacon until crisp, add mushrooms to spinach, pour bacon sippets and bacon fat over salad, add lemon, salt, pepper and herbs.

Fennel Salad

Serves 4

2 medium sized fennel roots
3 tbls olive oil
2 tbls lemon juice
¼ tsp crumbled thyme
1 tsp salt
1 tsp honey

Trim fennel roots, discarding tough outer leaves and reserving 2 feathery stems. Blend next 5 ingredients in a glass jar. Slice roots very thinly. Chop feathers. Pour dressing over roots and toss. Decorate with chopped fennel feathers. Allow to marinate at least 2 hours before serving. Excellent with spaghetti.

Snake Bean Salad

Serves 6

½ k snake beans
1 tsp salt
4 tbls olive or walnut oil
8 shallots, finely chopped
2 tbls snipped fresh dill
1 tbls tarragon vinegar
2 tinned red pimentos, diced
1-2 tbls pine nuts

Top and tail beans, slice into 4. Almost cover with boiling water, add salt. Boil briskly for 8 minutes. Strain into colander and allow cold tap water to run over them briefly. Place into salad bowl. Sprinkle with oil and toss well to coat beans. Add shallots and dill. Toss. Sprinkle with vinegar, toss and refrigerate for at least 30 minutes. Add pimentos and pine nuts, toss and serve.

Capsicums in Sour Cream

Serves 6-8

3 red capsicums
3 green capsicums
3 cloves garlic, halved
olive oil
salt and freshly ground pepper
lemon juice
sour cream

De-seed capsicums and slice into thin strips. Heat oil with garlic, add capsicum strips and allow to brown lightly, stirring occasionally to prevent burning. Remove to a bowl with slotted spoon. Discard garlic. Dust with salt and pepper, sprinkle with lemon juice. Stir in enough sour cream to coat lightly. Cool, cover and refrigerate. Toss again before serving.

Lebanese Salad

Serves 6

225 g burghul
225 g cooked, peeled prawns
225 g tomatoes, skinned, seeded and sliced
½ medium onion, grated
1 clove garlic, crushed
3 tbls parsley, finely chopped
1 tbls oil
1 tsp lemon rind, grated
2 tbls lemon juice
salt and freshly ground pepper

Pour 350 ml boiling water over burghul and allow to stand 30 minutes. Drain. Combine all remaining ingredients and chill to serve.

Beetroot and Apple Salad

Serves 6

½ k cooked beetroot, peeled and cubed while still warm
4 tbls lemon juice
½ tsp salt
freshly ground pepper ⎤— combine
½ cup vegetable oil ⎦
1 Roman lettuce
2 green apples, peeled, cored and cubed
½ cup crumbled blue vein cheese
½ cup walnuts, chopped
6 spring onions, finely sliced

Cook and prepare beetroot. Prepare dressing and shake in a bottle. Pour half dressing over warm beetroot and allow to rest at least 30 minutes. When salad is required tear lettuce into bite size pieces and place into a salad bowl. Coat with remaining dressing. Add apples, cheese, walnuts and onion. Fork beetroot through just before serving.

Salad Niçoise

Serves 6-8

4 tomatoes, quartered
1 medium onion, sliced thinly
1 yellow or red capsicum, cored
and cubed
12 radishes, sliced thinly
4 sticks celery, threaded and
chopped
1 tbls finely chopped basil
1 lettuce torn into bite size pieces
1 small tin tuna in oil
6 anchovy fillets, chopped
12 pimento stuffed olives, halved
¼ cup vinaigrette dressing
1 tbls capers
2-3 hard boiled eggs, quartered

Prepare vegetables and place into large salad bowl. Fork through tuna and its oil, anchovies and olives. Pour over vinaigrette dressing and toss well. Decorate top of bowl with eggs and capers to serve.

Fruited Slaw

Serves 4-6

4 tbls sultanas soaked in 4 tbls
dry white wine
½ medium sized Chinese
cabbage, shredded
3-4 red-skinned apples, cored and
thinly sliced
4 sticks celery, threaded and
chopped
2 tbls lemon juice
3 tbls chopped walnuts
4 tbls mayonnaise

Allow sultanas to soak in wine. Prepare cabbage, apples and celery and pile into large salad bowl. Sprinkle with lemon juice and walnuts. Remove sultanas with slotted spoon, add to salad and mix wine and mayonnaise; blend and fold into salad, mixing well.

Nutty Curly Lettuce Salad

Serves 6-8

3 heads endive
½ cup walnut pieces, chopped
½ cup wine vinegar
1 tbls Dijon mustard
salt and freshly ground pepper
¾ cup walnut oil

Tear lettuce into bite size pieces, wash and dry well. Place into salad bowl with nuts. Mix next 4 ingredients in a blender and pour over salad and toss.

Spanish Mixed Salad

Serves 6-8

3 anchovy fillets
1 clove garlic
¼ tsp salt
6 tbls olive oil
1 tbls grated onion
4 potatoes, cooked, cubed and
still warm
2 cups cooked green beans
1 tbls capers
1 tbls parsley, finely chopped
2 tomatoes, sliced
2 tbls tarragon vinegar
6-8 lettuce cups
6 stuffed green olives, sliced

Mash anchovy fillets with garlic and salt. Add olive oil and onion. Pour over cubed potatoes while still warm and mix well. Add beans, capers and parsley. Cool. Before serving add tomatoes, vinegar and toss well. Spoon into lettuce cups formed with leaves and decorate with olives.

Caesar Salad

Serves 4-6

1 large Cos lettuce
juice of ½ lemon
1 clove garlic, crushed
dash of Worcestershire sauce
4 tbls olive oil
1 very lightly boiled egg
3 slices bread, crusts removed
3-4 fillets anchovy, chopped
freshly ground black pepper
Parmesan cheese, grated

Tear lettuce, wash and dry well. Combine next 4 ingredients in a glass jar. Add egg and shake thoroughly. Cube bread, fry lightly with anchovies and their oil. Pour dressing over salad and toss. Dust with grinding of black pepper. Cover with fried croûtons while still warm and sprinkle salad with Parmesan cheese.

Chick Pea Salad

Serves 4

3 tbls olive oil
1 medium onion, finely chopped
2 cloves garlic, crushed
1 tin chick peas, drained
1 tomato, peeled and chopped
2 tbls parsley, finely chopped
salt and freshly ground pepper
½ cup chopped ham or garlic
sausage (optional)

Simmer onion and garlic in oil until soft but not coloured. Add chick peas, tomatoes, parsley and ham if used. Cover and simmer 10 minutes. Season to taste and serve hot or cold.

Celery and Kidney Bean Salad

Serves 4-6

1 large tin kidney beans
2 cups chopped celery, crisped in refrigerator
1 tbls finely chopped onion
½ cup chopped walnuts
¼ cup oil
3 tbls wine vinegar
salt and pepper

Drain beans and combine with celery, onions and nuts. Mix oil and vinegar, season and pour over beans. Chill and serve in lettuce cups.

OMELETTES

Successful omelettes require a certain amount of practice and a feather-light touch in preparation. I have a friend who, after a number of years of practice and some pretty solid tuition, still ends up with scrambled eggs!

The first important piece of equipment is a good omelette pan with a solid base and gently sloping sides. The second, a long, narrow and flexible spatula. Most people have a bowl of some sort but, without question, a copper or stainless steel bowl is best. *Never* use a rotary beater for mixing eggs for an omelette: a stainless steel whisk or a fork are the tools for this task.

After that come the ingredients: the eggs should be fresh and *never* used when straight out of the 'fridge. You may read all kinds of suggestions in various books about using milk or cream to blend the eggs. Toss the book out. Light omelettes should be made with eggs and water: preferably cooled boiled water in a ratio of 1 tablespoon of water for 2 eggs.

Cook omelettes in butter and *never* in oil. Heat your pan, put in a little butter and swirl it around. When the butter has foamed, turn the heat down a little and pour in the beaten eggs. Tilt the pan around so that the eggs spread evenly over the base of the pan. As the eggs begin to set, run the spatula around the edge of the omelette and loosen it to allow the remaining uncooked portion of egg to seep through and cook. In less than a minute the omelette will be cooked. The top should be moist if not runny. If you are preparing to fill the omelette, now is the time to get on with it. Your filling should be warm, unless it is just plain grated cheese. Quickly slip the spatula under the omelette and roll or fold it in half. The result should be tender and golden and must be served immediately.

Suggestions for filling omelettes

Fines herbes: for each omelette, chop finely 1 tsp parlsey, 1 tsp basil, 1 tsp dill. Mix with lightly whisked eggs before pouring into butter in fry pan. Roll omelette to serve. Herbs can be changed to suit seasons or availability, but endeavour not to mix herbs that are too pronounced in flavour and, when obliged to use dried herbs, remember that their flavour is more concentrated: so use half the recommended amount of fresh herbs. Fresh herbs are, of course, best.

Champignon: for each omelette allow ½ clove garlic crushed with a little salt to simmer lightly in 1 tbls butter. Add 4-6 button mushrooms, finely sliced, and stir to cook quickly. Remove and drain on kitchen paper. Add a little more butter to pan and quickly cook omelette. As it begins to set, top with mushrooms, sprinkle with 1 tsp finely minced parsley and roll omelette to serve.

Love Apple: for each omelette skin and de-seed 2 fresh tomatoes. Chop finely, season with salt, pepper and a squeeze of lemon juice. Dust with 1 tsp finely chopped basil and allow to steep for 20 minutes. Prepare omelette and, when beginning to set, cover with tomato mixture. Roll omelette while still firming and allow to heat through before serving.

Niçoise: warm through 2 tbls Ratatouille (recipe p. 64) per omelette. When egg is beginning to set spread mixture over half the omelette and fold. Dust with Parmesan cheese to serve.

Italien: for each omelette allow ½ clove garlic crushed with a little salt to simmer in 2 tbls butter. Quickly add 3 finely sliced zucchini and stir until glazed. Squeeze a little lemon juice over and, after 2 minutes, pour whisked eggs over zucchini. Allow eggs to almost set and fold over to serve.

Greek: slice 1 eggplant thinly, sprinkle with salt and allow to rest for 20 minutes. Rinse off salt, dry and dust lightly with flour. Melt 2 tbls butter in fry pan, add crushed clove of garlic and cook until golden. Discard garlic and fry 2 slices eggplant on both sides until golden, adding a little more butter if necessary. When both sides are cooked, cover with whisked eggs. Fold to serve, dust with Parmesan cheese; use remaining eggplant slices for individual omelettes.

Avocado: prepare Guacamole (recipe p. 8) and fill into omelettes just before rolling in pan; allow to warm through slightly.

Camembert Omelette

Serves 4

butter
8 eggs
4 tbls hot water
salt and freshly ground pepper
2 tbls basil, finely chopped
1 Camembert, cut into 4 equal
portions

Place walnut of butter into fry pan to heat. Whisk eggs with water, salt and pepper. Pour ¼ of the mixture into foaming butter and immediately add ¼ of basil and one ¼ of Camembert finely cubed. Lift egg mixture with spatula once it has set to allow remaining egg to cook through. Once beginning to set, roll omelette with aid of spatula and immediately lower heat. Rolling the omelette and lowering the heat will enable the cheese to melt. Place on a warm plate and serve immediately. Each omelette takes 2 minutes to cook. Decorate with a sprig of watercress to serve.

Spinach Omelette

Serves 2

250 g cooked spinach, puréed
4 eggs
2 tbls parsley, chopped
30 g butter
6 spring onions, chopped
30 g Cheddar cheese, finely
grated

Heat griller, whisk eggs with parsley and seasoning. Add spinach. Melt butter in omelette pan and cook onions over medium heat until tender. Raise heat and add egg and spinach mixture. Lift edges up to allow egg to cook. Slide onto plate, dust with cheese and brown lightly under griller to serve.

Anglers' Omelette

Serves 4

250 g fillets of fish
court bouillon to cover
1 k mussels
125 g mushrooms, sliced
1 glass dry white wine
1 tbls olive oil
1 tsp lemon juice
1 cup béchamel sauce
6 eggs
1 tbls dill, finely chopped
1 clove garlic, crushed with salt
walnut of butter

Poach fish in court bouillon and remove when tender (6 minutes at most). Remove skin, chop fish and reserve liquid. Steam mussels in minimum of water in a tightly closed pan (3 minutes). Discard any mussels not opened, remove remainder from shells, strain and reserve liquor. Sauté mushrooms in oil for 2 minutes, add wine and lemon juice. Béchamel sauce should now be prepared using reserved liquids. When ready, fold in fish, mussels and mushrooms. Whisk eggs, add dill and garlic. Heat butter in a large fry pan, when foaming add eggs, when nearly set, cover with warm fish mixture and fold. Serve immediately. Filling may be prepared in advance and re-heated over low flame while preparing omelette.

Tortilla Español (Spanish Omelette)

Serves 4

A Spanish tortilla is round, thick, golden brown on both sides and full of vegetables sautéed in oil. The only thing it has in common with an omelette is that it is also made of eggs. The tortilla is a meal in itself whether eaten hot or cold. It is taken to picnics in its cold state and eaten hot, whole or cut into wedges, for luncheon. I have lived in Spain and eaten many varieties over the years; although I offer you only the basic traditional recipe, I suggest you experiment with anything and everything that you have to hand once you have made the basic recipe. Tomatoes, eggplant, pimento, mushrooms, asparagus: everything tastes good when cooked in this fashion. Sharp garlic sausage, thinly sliced, ham or bacon are also good additions. The basis, however, has to be potato and onion.

1 large peeled potato, cut into small dice
1 large Spanish onion, chopped finely
3 tbls olive oil
5 eggs
salt and pepper to taste

Take a large fry pan and heat the oil. Sauté potato and onion until both are cooked but not browned; stir occasionally. Whisk eggs with seasoning and pour into pan spreading evenly. Cover with a lid, lower the heat, and allow the tortilla to cook for about 10 minutes. Take a plate of similar size to your fry pan and invert the tortilla; return immediately to fry pan and allow the other side to brown. The tortilla should be thick, golden and cooked through.

Omelette Provençale

Serves 6

This is a cold dish, ideal for picnics and other excursions; cut it into slices and serve with salad. Yummy!

4 medium onions
4 cloves
water to cover
1 tbls wine vinegar
1 tbls oil
8 eggs
salt, freshly ground pepper
1 tbls finely chopped basil

Peel onions. Pierce a hole into each one with the point of a sharp knife and insert cloves. Allow onions to soak in water and vinegar for 4 hours, then bring water to boil and cook for 10 minutes until tender. Drain and chop onions. Sauté them lightly in oil in a large fry pan. Whisk eggs, season, add basil. Add butter to onions. When melted, add eggs. Stir briefly, then allow to set by lowering heat and covering pan with a lid for a few minutes. Remove to a plate and allow to cool before refrigerating.

Omelette Soufflé

Serves 2

4 eggs
15 g flour
pinch salt
freshly ground pepper
25 g butter

Separate eggs. Add flour to beaten yolks and blend. Season with pinch pepper. Beat egg whites until stiff, add pinch salt. Very slowly fold yolks into egg whites. Melt butter in omelette pan and pour in egg mixture. Allow omelette to settle and turn golden. Place pan in preheated medium hot oven for 2 minutes. If desired, omelette can now have a hot filling poured over it, or it can be served plain.

Puffed Cheese and Walnut Omelette

Serves 1

2 eggs, separated
25 g grated cheese
1 tbls finely chopped walnuts
salt and pepper
butter for frying

Whisk egg whites until stiff. Combine yolks, cheese, nuts and seasoning. Fold gently into egg whites. Melt a little butter in a fry pan, pour in mixture and cook over medium heat until set and golden on the underside. Place pan briefly under pre-heated griller until puffed and serve immediately.

Farmers' Breakfast

Serves 2

Forget all you have learnt about preparing an omelette when making this substantial German-style omelette: good for a solid breakfast, a simple luncheon, or a great 'blotter' after a late night party. Great, too, for using up left-overs. If replacing the bacon with ham or cold meat, then it is necessary to fry the onion in a little butter first.

2 rashers bacon, diced
1 medium onion, thinly sliced
1-2 boiled potatoes, thinly sliced
3 mushrooms, sliced
2 zucchini, sliced
1 tomato, peeled and sliced
salt, pepper and paprika
1 tbls parsley, finely chopped
3 eggs
1 tbls water

Fry bacon. Add onion as fat melts from bacon. When golden but not brown, add potato and allow to colour. Add mushrooms, stir, cook 1 minute. Add zucchini, stir, cook 2 minutes. Add tomato, cook 2 minutes. Season and add parsley. Whisk eggs with water and pour over vegetables. As eggs begin to set, lift omelette with spatula and allow uncooked eggs to seep through and set. Lower heat, place a plate on top of pan for 1 minute which will help to set eggs, then serve on warmed plates.

VEGETABLE DISHES AND ACCOMPANIMENTS

In their raw state many protein foods are too hard to digest by the human digestive system. While cooking makes protein, fat and carbohydrate foods easier to digest, it can also destroy essential minerals and vitamins. To ensure a maximum intake of these it is essential to bear this in mind when planning a well balanced menu.

Most vegetables can be eaten in their raw state. For this select only tender young vegetables, and prepare them for eating as soon as possible after they have been picked. If you don't grow your own, their selection in the shop becomes even more important. Serve them as crudités, as the French call such a selection of raw vegetables. Arrange them attractively on a platter and offer a variety of dressings or sauces to dip them into. For example, skordalia is a Greek dressing (recipe p. 95) which is excellent for raw vegetables, and gives a change of flavour. A delicious start to any meal.

Remember not to overcook vegetables. Allow them to remain crisp on the palate, or 'al dente' as the Italians say. Vegetables contain a lot of water, so there is no need to use a lot to cook them. Drain them as soon as they are tender and never be tempted to add bicarbonate to green vegetables: it completely destroys their goodness. For best results vegetables should be steamed.

Melt a little butter to pour over cooked vegetables and change the flavour of the butter by the addition of some snipped herbs: basil, dill, fennel, all go well with vegetables. Add nuts to vegetables for yet another flavour, sesame seeds, sunflower seeds or pine nuts.

Prepare sauces to pour over lightly cooked vegetables. A fresh tomato sauce will give flavour as well as goodness to your vegetables, serve an orange sauce with carrots or broccoli, or prepare a Sabayon sauce for more festive occasions. You will find the recipes for these in the sauce section of this book.

Loudou's Indian Vegetable Curry with Rice and Dhall

Loudou's Indian Vegetable Curry (Chitchkee)

Serves 4

1/3 cup oil
2 tsp cummin
1/2 tsp turmeric
1/4 tsp chilli powder
1 tsp salt
2 large onions, chopped
2 cloves garlic, finely minced with small piece fresh ginger
2 large tomatoes, chopped
4 potatoes, quartered
1/4 head cauliflower, florets only
3-4 zucchini
1/2 eggplant
1 cup peas, shelled or frozen

Heat oil, stir in cummin, turmeric, chilli powder and salt. Add onions, cloves, garlic and ginger. Stir until glazed. Add all vegetables except peas and stir fry 5 minutes. Add 1/2 cup water and cover with a lid. Lower heat and simmer 20 minutes. Add peas and simmer 5 minutes more. Most of the moisture should be absorbed during cooking period. Serve with Indian rice, brinjal bhurta and dhal (recipe p. 60).

Brinjal Bhurta

2-3 eggplants
oil
3 tbls very finely minced onion
2 tbls dessicated coconut
salt
pinch chilli powder
1 small carton natural yoghurt

Anoint eggplants with oil and bake in a moderate oven. When soft, cool, and split open. Mash with remaining ingredients and chill before serving.

Vegetable and Nut Pie

Serves 4

1 large bunch spinach or silver beet
1 1/2 cups shallots, chopped
1 cup lettuce, shredded
1 cup parsley, chopped
1 tsp salt
1 1/2 tbls flour
1/4 tsp freshly ground pepper
1/2 cup walnuts
6 large eggs, beaten
3 tbls butter, melted
1 carton natural yoghurt

Wash spinach, remove large stems, chop leaves coarsely. Combine all vegetables with salt, flour, pepper and nuts. Mix eggs and pour butter into a pie plate. Spoon vegetable mixture into pie plate and bake in a moderate oven for 1 hour, until top is crisp and brown. Serve with yoghurt topping.

Vegetable Roulade

Serves 6

A roulade is like a Swiss roll. If this is the first time you've made one, I'm sure it won't be the last. I ate this one in America and found it very appetising and, if you have a food processor, this recipe will be a breeze.

½ k zucchini
¾ k eggplants
salt
2 tbls oil
½ k tomatoes
1 tbls sugar
1 tbls lemon juice
½ cup cream
salt and freshly ground pepper
2 tbls butter
2 onions
⅔ cup flour
1 cup warm milk
4 eggs, separated
½ cup Parmesan cheese, grated
fine dry breadcrumbs

Grate zucchini, sprinkle with salt and allow to rest in a colander. Peel and grate eggplant. Stirring, sauté in oil for 10 minutes. Peel tomatoes, process to liquid, add to eggplant with sugar and lemon juice. When mixture thickens add seasonings and cream. Melt butter in a separate pan, sauté onions until golden. Stir in flour and make a roux, gradually adding milk. Once thickened, remove from heat to cool. Beat egg yolks. Mix zucchini with Parmesan cheese, add egg yolks. Beat egg whites until stiff, gradually fold into zucchini mixture. Spread evenly on Swiss roll tin and bake at 200°C for 15 minutes. Turn out on a tea towel, spread with eggplant mixture, leaving a border of 3 cm along one side. Starting at this end, roll up lengthwise, using the towel to help in rolling. Return to the oven for 5 minutes to heat through.

Leek Roulade

Serves 6

3 leeks, sliced
4 eggs, separated
2 tbls Parmesan cheese, grated
2 tbls chives, chopped
60 g bacon, chopped
1 tbls butter
60 g mushrooms, chopped
1 tsp dry mustard

Line a Swiss roll tin with oiled greaseproof paper and heat oven to 200°C. Boil leeks in salt water for 3 minutes. Drain. Mix yolks of eggs with 1 tbls cheese, stir in leeks and chives. Beat egg whites until stiff. Fold whites into leek mixture. Spread mixture evenly over greaseproof paper, season with salt and bake for 15 minutes until firm. Meanwhile cook bacon in butter until browned, add mushrooms and cook 2 minutes. Stir in mustard. When leeks are cooked, spread this mixture over the top, sprinkle with remaining cheese and roll up as you would a Swiss roll.

Vegetable Strudel

Serves 6

2 medium carrots, thinly sliced
250 g butter or green beans
250 g broccoli flowers or chopped cabbage
1 leek
90 g butter
4 medium mushrooms
1 stick celery, finely chopped
125 g bean sprouts
salt and pepper
1 tbls fresh basil, finely chopped
fillo pastry
60 g melted butter
125 g grated Cheddar cheese mixed with 125 g fresh breadcrumbs

Slice carrots thinly and blanch 2 minutes in boiling salt water. Drain and set aside. Top, tail and slice beans. Cook 3 minutes in boiling salt water. Drain and set aside. Separate broccoli into florets and bring to the boil in salt water. Drain after 3 minutes. If using cabbage instead, just blanch lightly. Other vegetables may be used but do not overcook any of them. Slice leek very thinly and simmer in a little butter. When glazed add mushrooms. Cook 1 minute, add celery, stir, cook 1 minute. Add bean sprouts, stir, cook 1 minute. Add all other vegetables and stir to mix well. Allow to cool. Butter 5 leaves of filo pastry. Sprinkle mixed breadcrumbs. Top with vegetables and sprinkle with more crumbs. Season with salt, pepper and basil. Roll up, seal and brush with melted butter. Bake at 190° for 35 minutes. Serve with cheese or tomato sauce in a separate bowl. Strudel can be made in individual shapes by cutting fillo into squares. Centre vegetables and bring pastry up, twist to close.

Springtime Pudding

Serves 6

250 g asparagus spears, cut into 3
250 g peas
250 g baby carrots, halved
30 g butter
125 g button mushrooms, sliced
1 cup milk
100 g butter, melted
4 eggs, separated
1 tbls grated Parmesan cheese
1 tbls parsley, finely chopped
4 tbls dry breadcrumbs
1 tsp salt and freshly ground pepper

Blanch all vegetables except mushrooms separately in boiling salt water. Melt butter in a fry pan, cook mushrooms, parsley, and allow to simmer until all moisture has evaporated. Mix milk with melted butter, egg yolks and breadcrumbs. Add blanched vegetables, mushrooms, and stir. Beat egg whites until stiff. Fold into mixture. Butter a pyrex dish and pour in mixture. Bake, uncovered, in a medium oven for 30 minutes. Allow to rest for 5 minutes before turning out on a serving plate.

German Potato Pancakes

Serves 8

2 k potatoes
3 eggs, beaten
1 cup flour
milk
½ cup parsley, chopped finely
1 tsp salt
freshly ground pepper
butter

Peel potatoes and grate them. Mix eggs with flour and stir in potatoes with enough milk to bind and make a thick batter. Add parsley and season. Melt 1 tbls butter in a fry pan, add sufficient batter to cover base and cook over moderate heat until set and golden. Turn with spatula and cook the other side. Keep warm in low oven and repeat with remaining batter, making 8 pancakes. Top with vegetable purée as suggested on page 94 or serve topped with fried onions, mushrooms or tomatoes.

Savoury Brussels Sprouts Pudding

Serves 6

½ k brussels sprouts
1 cup milk
4 tbls flour
4 eggs, separated
4 tbls grated Cheddar cheese
100 g butter

Sauce:
1 cup sour cream
1 egg yolk
½ cup milk
salt

Cook sprouts in boiling salt water until almost tender. Strain and drain thoroughly. Heat milk, add butter, flour, egg yolks and last of all cheese. Carefully fold in sprouts and allow mixture to cool. Beat egg whites until stiff and fold into cooled sprouts mixture. Pour into oiled pudding basin and cover firmly. Place basin into large saucepan containing enough boiling water to reach half way up the side of the basin. Cook for 1 hour. Allow basin to rest for 10 minutes before turning out. In the meantime, prepare sauce by mixing sour cream with egg yolk. Add milk and cook, stirring constantly, until mixture just begins to boil. Remove from heat and season to taste. Serve sauce separately.

Beetroot Timbale

Serves 6-8

6 medium sized beetroot, cooked
4 medium sized onions, grated
3 tbls butter
2½ tbls flour
3 chicken stock cubes mixed with
½ cup hot water
½ cup cream, warmed
2 tbls chopped chives or dill
nutmeg
salt and freshly ground pepper
3 whole eggs
1 additional egg yolk
½ cup sour cream mixed with 3 tbls chopped chives, for filling

Preheat oven to 190°C and butter a ring mould. Peel beetroot while still warm, chop and place into a food processor to purée with metal blade. Set aside in separate bowl. Use grater to prepare onions. Melt butter and simmer onion lightly but do not brown. Stir in flour and make a roux. Take off heat and stir in chicken stock, then cream, and return to heat to cook flour, stirring constantly. Remove from heat, stir in beetroot and season with chives, nutmeg, salt and pepper. Lightly whisk whole eggs with additional egg yolk and blend into beetroot mixture. Fill into buttered mould. Set mould into a baking dish filled with water to come half way up side of mould. Place into oven for 35 minutes. Test with knife: if it comes out cleanly, timbale is ready to remove from oven. Allow to rest for 10 minutes then turn out onto serving platter. Fill centre with warmed sour cream mixed with chives and slice to serve.

Eggplant Casserole

Serves 6

3 eggplants
1 cup dry breadcrumbs
1 cup grated firm Cheddar cheese
¼ cup butter
salt and freshly ground pepper
250 g mushrooms, sliced thickly
1 litre fresh tomato sauce

Cover eggplants with boiling salt water, reduce heat and simmer 10 minutes. Drain and cool. Quarter lengthwise, then cut crosswise and remove peel. Mix breadcrumbs with cheese and layer in a deep casserole eggplants, mushrooms and tomato sauce. Sprinkle with cheese, dot with butter and sprinkle with salt and pepper. Bake uncovered in a moderate oven for 25 minutes.

Hungarian Vegetable Loaf

Serves 6-8

350 g borlotti beans
1 bay leaf
350 g soya beans
2 medium onions, finely chopped
4 cloves garlic
1 capsicum, seeded and diced
2 eggs, beaten
1 tbls oil
1 cup breadcrumbs
1 tbls chopped parsley
1½ bunches spinach
100 g roasted unsalted peanuts,
blended in machine with 1
medium sized can button
mushrooms, drained and chopped
1-2 fresh chillies, seeded and
chopped
1 small tin poivre vert
1-2 tbls paprika
salt, pepper and cayenne to taste

Soak beans overnight in water, then boil in salt water with bay leaf. When cooked, purée beans in blender with a little cooking liquid. Add onions, garlic and capsicum. Blend in eggs, oil, breadcrumbs and parsley. Add seasoning to taste. Steam spinach. When tender, purée and add peanut mixture, chillies and poivre vert. Place bean mixture on a floured board, flatten to thickness of 4 cm with a rolling pin. Top with spinach mixture in the centre and fold bean mixture over to form a loaf. Sprinkle liberally with paprika, then place in a buttered ovenproof dish and bake at 190° for 1 hour. Loaf may be served hot or cold.

Cabbage Cake

Serves 4

This splendid cake looks and tastes very good and is well worth the little extra trouble it takes to make. Any variety of green vegetables in season may be used.

4 large green cabbage leaves to
line a 15 cm cake tin
3 cups chopped green vegetables,
such as spinach, sorrel, Chinese
cabbage, leeks, onions, spring
onions
1 tbls herbs, such as tarragon,
chives, parsley
1 egg
1 egg white
2 tbls plain yoghurt
2 tbls cottage cheese
salt and pepper

Remove thick stalks of whole cabbage leaves and blanch 2-3 minutes in boiling salt water. Drain. Blanch green vegetables 2-3 minutes. Drain. Blanch onions and leeks 3-4 minutes. Drain. Line cake tin with cabbage leaves, tips to meet in centre, allowing base of leaves to hang over edge of tin, able to cover contents once filling has been added. Fill with blanched vegetables. Fork egg and egg white together, add yoghurt, cream cheese, herbs and seasonings. Pour over filling and bring up cabbage leaves to close. Cover with foil and bake in a baking dish half filled with water for 1 hour. Remove and allow to rest 15 minutes before turning out of cake tin. Slice and serve with fresh tomato sauce.

VEGETABLE ACCOMPANIMENTS

Pickled Pumpkin Balls

These are delicious served with brussels sprouts. Use a melon baller and scoop out enough balls from a pumpkin to make 2 cups full. Reheat prepared pumpkin balls briefly with sprouts when they are cooked.

Combine:
2 cups sugar
1 cup cider vinegar
½ cup water
1 cinnamon stick, crumbled
6 cloves
½ tsp allspice
4 strips thinly pared lemon peel

Bring the mixture to the boil, washing down any sugar crystals clinging to sides of pan with a brush dipped in cold water. When sugar dissolves, simmer for 5 minutes without stirring. Add pumpkin and simmer 15 minutes. Transfer pumpkin to a jar with slotted spoon. Reduce syrup to half and pour over pumpkin. Cool, cover and store.

Rosy Dhal

Pulse foods are eaten throughout India and Asia and contain the highest protein value known to man. There are innumerable recipes for dhal but this is my favourite.

500 g yellow lentils
2-3 onions, finely sliced
2-3 tomatoes, skinned and chopped
1 tsp chilli powder
2 tsp turmeric
1 tsp salt
2 tbls tomato paste

Soak lentils in water to cover for 30 minutes. Fry onion until glazed. Add tomatoes, chilli, turmeric and salt. Cook and stir 5 minutes. Bring lentils to the boil, stir in onion mixture, lower heat and simmer 1 hour. Stir in tomato paste. This delicious vegetable dish can be served with any meal but it is, of course, best served with curry and rice. For special occasions top and tail green capsicums and de-seed. Blanch them briefly in boiling salt water. Remove with a slotted spoon and drain. Fill cavities with dhal.

Hungarian Marrow Purée

1 k marrow
1 tbls salt
60 g butter
1 tbls flour
½ tsp paprika
2 tbls fresh dill, finely chopped
1 tsp sugar
½ cup sour cream

Peel marrow, cut in two, scrape inside and cut marrow into thin strips. Place in a bowl and sprinkle with salt. Allow to stand 30 minutes. Drain and squeeze marrow juice out with hands. Melt butter in a saucepan, stir in flour to make a roux. Take from heat, stir in dill and paprika, add marrow and ½ cup water. Return to heat, stir and simmer for 20 minutes. Add sugar, sour cream, and cook 5 minutes more before serving.

Rosy Dhal served in Green Capsicums

Baked Zucchini in Sour Cream

½ k zucchini
90 g cream cheese
2 tbls onion, finely chopped
½ tsp salt and freshly ground
pepper
½ carton sour cream
paprika

Place zucchini in boiling salt water, reduce heat and simmer 5 minutes. Drain, cut in half lengthwise, scoop seeds into a small bowl. Mix these with cream cheese, onion and seasoning. Fill into zucchini and arrange in buttered casserole. Spoon some sour cream over zucchini, dust with paprika and bake in a shallow greased baking dish, uncovered, for 8-10 minutes to heat through.

Chinese Braised Vegetables

2 tbls peanut oil
1 tsp sesame oil
1 clove garlic, crushed
1 tsp fresh grated ginger
½ k sliced vegetables, mixed
½ cup hot water
1 tbls oyster sauce
½ tsp salt
½ tsp monosodium glutamate
2 tsp cornflour
1 tbls water

In a wok heat oil with garlic and ginger. Add vegetables and stir fry 2 minutes. Add hot water, sauce, salt and monosodium glutamate. Simmer 4 minutes. Push vegetables to one side of wok, add cornflour mixed with water and stir until thick. Fork vegetables through thickened sauce and serve with boiled rice.

Sesame Potatoes

½ k potatoes, well mashed
6 black olives, stoned and
chopped
1 tsp finely chopped basil
1 tsp salt
2 tbls butter, melted
2 tbls fresh breadcrumbs
125 g sesame seeds
vegetable oil for shallow frying

Cook potatoes and mash. Place into a bowl and mix with olives, basil, salt, butter and breadcrumbs. Blend well and form into patties. Press each patti into sesame seeds and fry on both sides until golden. Serve with one or more vegetable dishes, or top with a vegetable purée to serve.

Chinese Braised Vegetables served
with Rice

Onion Ragoût

4 tbls butter
1 k small onions
3 tbls white wine
2 cloves
small stick cinnamon
1 bay leaf
1¼ cups chicken stock, made with
cubes
1 small can tomatoes, sieved

Melt butter in a heavy based saucepan and fry whole onions until golden brown. Add all remaining ingredients and simmer for 45 minutes until onions are tender.

Ratatouille

6 large zucchini
3 small eggplants
salt and pepper
1 cup olive oil
2 large onions, sliced
4 cloves garlic, chopped
2 green capsicums, seeded and
sliced thinly
8 tomatoes, skinned and chopped

Peel and slice eggplant and zucchini. Sprinkle eggplant with salt and allow to rest 20 minutes. Wash salt off and wipe dry. Heat oil in a heavy pan and fry onions until golden. Add garlic and capsicum. Fry 5 minutes. Add tomatoes and cook 5 minutes. Add zucchini and eggplant. Season to taste and simmer gently for 45 minutes. Place into sterilized jar when cool and seal, or place into a shallow casserole dish, sprinkle with grated Parmesan cheese and allow to brown under the grill before serving as a vegetable course. Ratatouille is also good as a filling for omelettes.

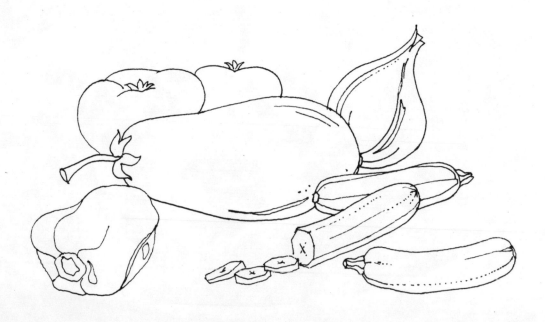

EGG DISHES

Perhaps the most spectacular egg dish is a soufflé. In restaurants these always seem to be the most expensive dishes on the menu. Somewhat startling when you think about it. Basically a soufflé is made up of left-overs, bound together in a béchamel sauce, and the whole thing is made light and puffy with the help of some well beaten egg whites. Nothing to be afraid of. To be sure, the balance of quantities to be used is important. After all there are only a few egg whites to hold it all up!

To make a successful soufflé you must first have a good oven. A temperamental one won't do. Then you need a proper soufflé dish with straight sides so that the mixture can climb up. Always *fold* the stiff egg whites into your mixture very lightly so that they are blended but no trapped air is lost. If you are making a soufflé for the first time, fill your soufflé dish three quarters full: it's easier than trying to tie a paper collar on the dish and your mixture will still rise attractively over the top of the bowl. Admittedly a collar looks stunning when you take it off but, until you are an expert, you won't have to worry about the overflow burning on the base of your oven. Soufflés are nice starters for a meal whether they are cooked in individual dishes or in a large one. They also make an excellent main event. Once cooked they must be served immediately.

A quiche can provide a satisfactory luncheon dish or it can also be an appetising starter. It has the advantage over a soufflé in so far as it can be made in advance, kept in the fridge and reheated in a moderate oven when required. I am a little bored with quiche lorraine so I tend to try different fillings, as I am sure you will once you have experimented with a few suggestions.

One small word of advice, serve only one egg dish at any one meal. Eggs are substantial fare and only hens are meant to sit on them!

Surprise Cheese Soufflé

Serves 6

This soufflé offers a contrast to the usual cheese soufflé because the diced, cold Camembert will not be completely melted when the soufflé is cooked, but slightly runny — which is quite a sensation!

2 tbls butter
2 tbls flour
300 ml warmed milk
4 egg yolks, lightly beaten
125 g Gruyère cheese, grated
salt
freshly ground white pepper
dash cayenne
1 tbls French mustard
1 small, cold, tinned Camembert cheese, diced
5 egg whites, whisked until stiff
Parmesan cheese

Preheat oven to 200°C. Melt butter over medium heat and stir in flour to make a roux. Remove from heat, stir in milk and return to stove, stirring constantly. Cook until thickened, remove from heat and stir in egg yolks. Add Gruyère, stir well and season with next 4 ingredients. Allow to cool a little while dicing Camembert and whipping egg whites. Butter and prepare a large soufflé dish, sprinkle lightly with Parmesan. If you wish to prepare a soufflé in advance for a dinner party the dish can be prepared up to this point and left until 35 minutes before you wish to serve it. Add stiff egg whites to mixture, fold in diced Camembert and pour mixture into prepared dish. Sprinkle top lightly with 1 tbls Parmesan cheese and place into oven. Do not disturb for 30 minutes, then serve immediately.

Spinach Soufflé

Serves 6

1 tbls butter
3 spring onions, finely chopped
1 pkt frozen spinach purée, defrosted
6 tbls butter
5 tbls flour
1 tsp salt
good grating of pepper
¼ tsp grated nutmeg
6 egg yolks
7 egg whites
grated Parmesan cheese

Preheat oven to 220°C. Butter a large soufflé dish and dust lightly with Parmesan cheese. Melt 1 tbls butter and briefly sauté onions. When glazed, stir in spinach and cook for 5 minutes until all moisture has evaporated. Season with salt, pepper and nutmeg and set aside. Melt butter over low heat and make a roux with flour, stirring until smooth. Add spinach to roux, stirring constantly. Remove from heat and stir in well beaten egg yolks and allow to cool. Beat egg whites until stiff, fold into spinach mixture and pour into prepared soufflé dish. Sprinkle with Parmesan and bake for 40 minutes until the top is puffy and nicely browned.

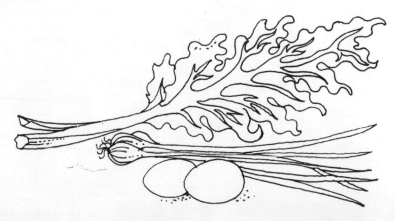

Cheese soufflé

Broccoli Soufflé

Serves 6

3 tbls butter
3 tbls flour
1½ cups warm milk
5 egg yolks, beaten
1½ cups steamed broccoli,
chopped
½ cup chopped walnuts
2 tbls finely chopped onion
2 tbls grated Parmesan cheese
½ tsp salt and freshly ground
pepper
freshly grated nutmeg
7 egg whites, stiffly beaten

Butter a large soufflé dish, sprinkle with a little grated Parmesan cheese and tie a buttered collar round the dish if you wish. Melt butter, stir in flour to make a roux. Remove from heat and stir in warm milk. Return to heat and allow to thicken and cook flour, stirring constantly. When smooth, remove from heat and gradually whisk in egg yolks. Add broccoli and chopped nuts. Stir in onion and cheese. Adjust seasoning. If you are entertaining guests, your mixture can be prepared in advance up to this point. An hour before required, whisk egg whites until stiff, lightly fold into broccoli mixture. Pour into prepared soufflé dish and bake in a preheated 190°C oven for 40 minutes. Serve immediately. A fresh tomato sauce (p. 94) can be served separately.

Note: Two more soufflé recipes are featured in this book in the pasta section, p. 71.

Pumpkin Quiche Soufflé

Serves 6

Pastry:
1½ cups flour
3 tbls butter
2 tbls lard
½ tsp salt
2 tbls cold water

Filling:
500 g butternut pumpkin
1 tbls butter
10 shallots, finely sliced
salt
pinch nutmeg and ginger
3 eggs, separated
¼ cup cream

Work butter and lard into flour until mixture resembles crumbs, add salt and water, form into a ball and allow to rest in refrigerator for 30 minutes. Roll out and fit into 23 cm flan dish with removable ring. Return to refrigerator for another 30 minutes. Prick base, line with foil, rice or beans, and bake blind for 15 minutes.

Prepare pumpkin and cook until tender. Drain well and mash. Melt butter and cook shallots until tender. Add to mashed pumpkin with salt, nutmeg and ginger. Beat egg yolks and add. Beat in cream. Whisk egg whites until stiff, fold into pumpkin and pour into prepared pastry. Bake in a preheated 190°C oven for 30 minutes until well-risen and cooked. This quiche must be served straight from the oven.

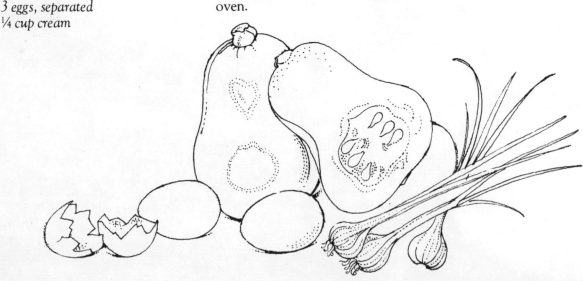

Quiche Niçoise

Quiche Niçoise

Serves 6-8

Prepare pastry as for previous receipe and bake blind as before.

Filling:
1 cup onion, finely sliced
2 tbls oil
½ cup ham, sliced and cubed
1 cup tomatoes, peeled, seeded and chopped
½ cup green capsicum, diced
1 tbls capers
1 tbls basil, finely chopped
salt and freshly ground pepper
½ cup cream
3 eggs
½ cup cheddar cheese, grated
12 olives, stuffed and halved

Simmer onions in oil until tender but not coloured. Add ham, simmer 2 minutes. Add tomatoes, simmer 4 minutes. Add capsicum, capers, basil and season to taste. Cook, stirring occasionally, until most of the juice has evaporated then set aside to cool. Beat cream and eggs, add cooled filling and grated cheese. Pour into pastry, decorate with olives and dot with a few pieces of butter. Bake in a moderate oven for 30 minutes. Cool slightly before cutting.

Egg and Spinach Tart

Serves 6-8

Pastry as for Pumpkin Quiche Soufflé

Filling:
3 tbls shallots, chopped
2 tbls butter
1½ cups spinach cooked and drained, or frozen
dash of nutmeg
salt and freshly ground pepper
250 g cream cheese
4 eggs, separated
½ cup cream

Blend first 5 ingredients over medium heat for 5 minutes. Place into a bowl and add cream cheese. Separate eggs, add 4 yolks, one at a time, to spinach. Add cream. Whisk egg whites in another bowl until stiff, then fold into spinach mixture. Remove rice and paper from flan case, fill with spinach mixture. Dot with butter and bake for 20 minutes in a medium oven. Allow to cool slightly before slicing to serve.

Mexican Eggs

Serves 6

2 medium onions, finely chopped
1 tbls oil
1 tin Mexican red chilli sauce
½ cup tomato sauce
½ tsp oregano
1 tin refried beans
1 tbls butter
½ cup grated Cheddar cheese
6 hot fried tortillas
6 eggs
1 avocado, sliced

Cook onion in oil until soft, add chilli sauce, tomato sauce and oregano. Simmer uncovered for 10 minutes, stirring occasionally. Place beans into shallow casserole, dot with butter, sprinkle with cheese. Bake in a moderate oven for 10 minutes. Fry tortillas, place on plates, top with tomato mixture, and keep warm. Fry eggs, place on top of tortillas, add sliced avocado and serve with refried beans.

PASTA

There is a seemingly endless variety of pasta on the market and all of it can be served either as a starter to a meal or as a main course. Pasta is delicious even when only simply dressed with oil and garlic, or anointed with butter and finely chopped fresh basil, or even just topped with grated Parmesan cheese. The larger varieties can be stuffed and baked or even fried. The smaller and more delicate varieties are best served with imaginative sauces. Which reminds me to add, never swamp your pasta in sauce, always remember that the pasta is meant to be the main event and the sauce the decoration.

If you own a food processor you can prepare your own fresh pasta in minutes. Rolling it out thinly is a little more trouble so, if you enjoy eating pasta often, buying a pasta machine is a good investment. It removes any vestiges of hard work. There are several machines on the market to choose from and home-made pasta, when fresh, takes only minutes to cook. When using bought pasta, only buy the best.

There are a few tricks in preparing good pasta. First of all, the amount of water used for cooking is of primary importance. Use a large saucepan with lots of water for the pasta to move around in. Put 2 tablespoons of salt into the water for every 450 g of pasta. Allow the water to boil briskly for 2 minutes before adding the pasta. Stir occasionally to prevent it from sticking together. Never overcook pasta: it should be slightly chewy or 'al dente', as the Italians say — 'on the tooth'. Test by lifting one piece of pasta out of the saucepan with a fork, then squeeze it between index finger and thumb: if it separates it is cooked. Cooking time varies with brands, but a good guide for beginners is as follows:

Spaghetti: 12 minutes
Thin varieties: 10 minutes
Macaroni: 12-15 minutes
Noodles: 10 minutes

Before draining cooked pasta, pour some cold water into the saucepan to stop the water from boiling: this removes some of the starch. Then drain it in a colander and serve as you wish.

Home-made Pasta

Serves 4

185 g plain flour
1 egg
1 egg white
1 tbls iced water
1 tbls olive oil

Place flour and salt into food processor with dough blade. While motor runs pour egg mixture through funnel. As mixture comes together add water and oil. Use pulse switch for 4–5 minutes to knead pasta. If mixture is too wet and sticks to bowl, sprinkle with a little extra flour. If mixture is too crumbly and not coming together, add a few drops of water.

If you have a small capacity bowl on your processor, once mixture comes together, divide and knead each half for 4 minutes. Pasta will be hot and elastic, so leave to cool in refrigerator for 10 minutes. Divide mixture in half. Sprinkle board and rolling pin with flour and roll out first half as thinly as possible. Repeat with other half, pulling and stretching as you go.

This quantity is sufficient for 4 servings, all your processor will handle at one time. Extra quantities can, of course, be made.

Note: if green pasta is required, omit iced water and add 30 g frozen spinach and use only ½ tbls oil.

Tagliatelle Soufflé

Serves 4

500 g home-made tagliatelle
90 g butter
1½ tsp flour
450 ml milk
6 tbls grated Parmesan cheese
salt, freshly ground pepper and nutmeg
4 eggs, separated

This recipe should be made only with home-made tagliatelle. Cook as directed but remember that freshly made pasta takes only 5 minutes to cook. Make a roux from butter and flour, remove from heat and stir in milk. Return to heat and allow to thicken. Season with salt, pepper and nutmeg. Stir in cheese and remove from heat. Whisk yolks lightly and add to sauce. Whip egg whites until stiff and fold into the cooled sauce. Make sure pasta is well-drained and fold into sauce. Pour into a buttered soufflé dish lightly dusted with additional 1 tbls grated Parmesan cheese. Bake in a moderate oven for 20 minutes. Serve immediately.

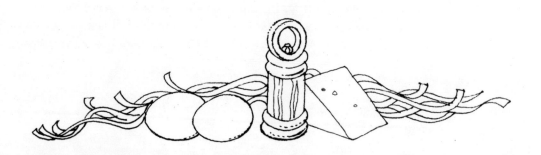

SAUCE SUGGESTIONS FOR PASTA

Milanese Sauce

½ cup finely chopped onion
2 tbls olive oil
1 small tin anchovy fillets
120 g tin tomato paste
1 litre water
2 tbls pine nuts

Sauté onion in olive oil until golden. Add anchovies and their oil. Mash to a paste with a wooden spoon. Add tomato paste and water. No need to season as the anchovies do that. Add pine nuts and cook over low heat, stirring frequently until sauce is thick.

Ricotta Sauce

1 small onion, chopped
4 tbls olive oil
450 g ricotta cheese
1 tin tomato purée
½ small tin tomato paste
600 ml water
salt and pepper

Lightly fry onion in oil until golden. Add ricotta, stir in tomato purée, paste and water to blend. Mix with a wooden spoon until cheese resembles coarse sand. Season to taste and cook slowly over a low flame for 45 minutes. Pour over pasta. Grated Parmesan cheese can be sprinkled over finished dish if desired.

Tomato and Basil Cream Sauce

6 tomatoes, peeled
3 tbls butter
2 cloves garlic, crushed
½ tsp salt
2 tbls fresh basil, chopped
1 tbls flour
1 cup cream
1 tbls tomato paste
1 glass dry white wine

Place skinned tomatoes in a blender and purée. Melt 2 tbls butter in a pan and sauté garlic briefly. Add tomato pulp, salt and basil. Reduce to half over medium heat. In a saucepan melt remaining butter, stir in flour to make a roux with cream. Add tomato paste, stir, add wine. Combine with reduced tomato mixture and serve.

Salsa Verde (Green Sauce)

*handful of parsley, stalks
removed
4 anchovy fillets
2 tbls fresh breadcrumbs
1 small onion
1 small gherkin
2 cloves garlic
freshly ground black pepper
olive oil
2 tbls wine vinegar*

Place first 6 ingredients into a blender or food processor and whisk briefly. Add good grinding of black pepper. Gradually add oil as if for mayonnaise. Finish with vinegar.

Tuna and Olive Sauce

*1 cup tomato sauce (recipe p.94)
125 g black olives
6–8 anchovy fillets
1 medium sized tin of tuna in oil
freshly ground black pepper
squeeze of lemon juice*

Warm prepared tomato sauce. Stone and chop olives. Mash anchovies, add to tuna and combine. Stir both into tomato sauce to heat through. Finish with a little black pepper and a squeeze of lemon juice.

Tagliatelle Pudding

Serves 8

250 g white tagliatelle
125 g green tagliatelle
2 medium tomatoes, peeled and
puréed
1 tbls chopped fresh basil
125 g Mozzarella cheese
125 g ricotta cheese
butter
Parmesan cheese, grated

Cook white tagliatelle as directed and strain in a colander. Cook green tagliatelle in the same manner. Prepare tomatoes. Butter a large round Pyrex dish and dust with Parmesan cheese. Cover with a layer of white tagliatelle. Top with a layer of mozarella cheese. Cover with another layer of white tagliatelle. Pour tomatoes over, sprinkle with basil and freshly ground pepper. Top with a layer of green tagliatelle. Top with a layer of ricotta cheese and some more pepper. Finish off with a layer of white tagliatelle. Dot generously with butter, sprinkle with Parmesan cheese, cover with foil and bake in a medium hot oven for 30 minutes. Turn out and serve with extra fresh tomato sauce (recipe p. 94) and a salad.

Baked Cannelloni

Serves 6 as an entrée

When cooking cannelloni always add 1 tbls oil to the boiling salted water, the oil will prevent the cannelloni tubes sticking together. Cannelloni can be served as an appetiser or as a main event accompanied by a scrumptious salad.

12 cannelloni tubes
2 tbls oil
1 onion, chopped finely
200 g ricotta cheese
4 tbls walnuts, chopped
1 tbls tomato paste
1 tsp basil
1 tsp sugar
10 stuffed olives
salt and pepper

Sauce:
300 ml béchamel sauce
1 tsp made mustard
2 tbls tomato paste
½ cup grated cheese

Blanch cannelloni for 5 minutes in boiling salt water with 1 tbls oil. Drain and refresh under running cold water until cool. Heat oven to 190°C. Heat oil in frying pan and fry onion until soft. Stir into ricotta cheese, add walnuts and tomato paste with basil, sugar and chopped olives. Season and fill into cannelloni. Place into shallow ovenproof dish. Prepare sauce, adding most of the cheese but reserving a little for sprinkling on top. Pour sauce over cannelloni, sprinkle with cheese and bake in a moderate oven for 20 minutes.

Cannelloni Crisps

Serves 4

8 tubes cannelloni
1 tbls oil
1 red capsicum, seeded and
chopped finely
1 cup chopped mushrooms
300 ml béchamel sauce (recipe
p. 00)
salt and freshly ground white
pepper
50 g fresh breadcrumbs
50 g flour
1 egg, beaten
100 g fine breadcrumbs
oil for frying

Cook cannelloni for 5 minutes in boiling salt water with 1 tbls oil. Drain and refresh under running cold water. Heat oil in fry pan and cook capsicum until soft. Add mushrooms and fry 3 more minutes. Heat béchamel sauce, stir in onion and mushrooms. Mix in breadcrumbs and seasonings. Fill cannelloni with sauce, dredge lightly in flour and then coat with beaten egg and breadcrumbs. Chill for 1 hour. When required, heat oil and fry cannelloni until golden. Delicious served with ratatouille (recipe p. 64).

Cauliflower and Macaroni Soufflé

Serves 4-6

1 medium cauliflower
2 tsp made mustard
5 eggs, separated
salt and pepper
300 ml béchamel sauce
100 g grated Cheddar cheese
100 g elbow macaroni, cooked al
dente

Break cauliflower into florets and trim stalks to similar sized pieces. Boil until tender in salt water. Drain, mash and purée. Add mustard, egg yolks, season with salt and pepper. Add grated cheese to béchamel sauce, cool and add sauce to purée. Blend in cooked macaroni. Beat egg whites until stiff and fold in gently. Spoon into large greased souffle dish and bake for 35 minutes in a pre-heated oven at 190°C. Serve immediately.

Seafood Macaroni

Serves 4-6

24 mussels, well washed and
scraped
1 cup dry white wine
salt and freshly ground pepper
500 g large peeled prawns
225 g sliced mushrooms
50 g butter
12 shallots, finely sliced
bouquet garni
¼ tsp paprika
2 tbls brandy (optional)
225 g macaroni
150 ml tomato sauce
150 ml bechamel sauce
pinch cayenne pepper

Place mussels into pan with wine and pepper, simmer 5 minutes. Strain liquid and reserve. Remove mussels from shells. Fry mushrooms in butter, remove with a slotted spoon and keep warm. Brown shallots in same butter, add prawns, bouquet garni and paprika. Cook 7 minutes. If using brandy add now and flame. Douse with reserved mussel liquid and simmer further 5 minutes. Remove prawns and keep warm. Cook macaroni in boiling salt water and drain. Allow mussel liquid to reduce to half then add mussels and prawns. Remove bouquet garni and pour sauce over macaroni.

Salmon Noodle Casserole

Serves 6

1 large tin salmon or tuna
250 g thin noodles
3 tbls butter
3 tbls flour
½ tsp salt and freshly ground
pepper
liquid from salmon and milk to
make 2 cups liquid
250 g mushrooms, thinly sliced
3 tbls butter
125 g grated Cheddar cheese
paprika to garnish

Drain salmon, reserve liquid and remove bones. Flake coarsely. Cook noodles in boiling salt water. Oil casserole. In a saucepan melt butter, blend in flour to make a roux with salmon liquid and milk mixture, stirring constantly. Season. Sauté mushrooms lightly in butter, stir in flour, then add flaked salmon and sauce. Drain and place noodles in buttered casserole, pour mixture over and sprinkle lightly with cheese. Dust with paprika and brown under griller until bubbly.

Cheese and Spinach Gnocchi

Potato Gnocchi

Serves 6

1 k potatoes
4 tbls butter
½ cup flour
3 eggs, beaten
½ cup grated Cheddar cheese
salt, pepper and nutmeg
additional butter, melted
grated Parmesan cheese

Boil potatoes in their jackets until tender. Peel and mash them with butter. Gradually beat in flour. Add eggs, then cheese, beating continuously. Season with salt, pepper and nutmeg. The dough should be soft and manageable. Shape into long cylinders with floured hands. With a sharp knife, cut into shapes like small scones. In a large saucepan bring salted water to the boil and drop gnocchi in to cook for 8 minutes. Remove with a slotted spoon and drain. Place into buttered, shallow casserole, drizzle with melted butter and sprinkle with Parmesan cheese. Place into pre-heated oven at 190°F for 10-15 minutes until lightly browned. Gnocchi can be prepared well in advance for a dinner party entrée with a minimum of labour.

Alternatives: omit butter and cheese when placing in the oven and cover with a tomato or mushroom sauce. Gnocchi can also be served cold when there are left-overs; simply cover with French dressing, finely chopped shallots and diced pimento.

Cheese and Spinach Gnocchi

Serves 6

250 g spinach leaves
6 tbls butter, melted
500 g ricotta cheese
⅓ cup grated Parmesan cheese
3 egg yolks, beaten
6 tbls flour
1 tsp salt
freshly ground pepper and pinch
of nutmeg
grated Parmesan for dusting
½ cup tomato sauce

Wash and tear spinach. Cook for 3 minutes in 3 tbls melted butter over medium high heat. Shake pan to prevent sticking. All liquid should evaporate before spinach is puréed. Cool and combine with ricotta and Parmesan cheese. Add beaten egg yolks, stir in flour and season. Stir vigorously or use blender. Chill mixture for at least 30 minutes. Heat a large saucepan of salt water. Meanwhile prepare gnocchi by using 2 teaspoons to form mixture into small egg-shapes. Roll shapes lightly in flour. When all the mixture is used up cook gnocchi a few at a time in simmering salt water for 12 minutes. Make sure they do not stick to each other. Remove with a slotted spoon and place them into a shallow casserole brushed with melted butter. Pour tomato sauce over, dust with extra Parmesan cheese and bake at 190°C for 15 minutes until cheese begins to colour.

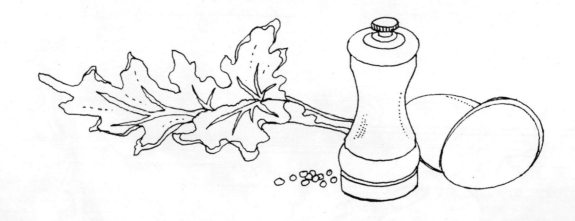

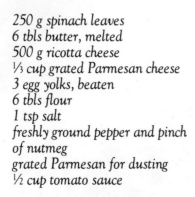

RICE

Rice, which originated in China and India, is the staple food of two thirds of the world's population. Every country has its own favourite way of cooking it. The type of rice you buy will largely influence the method you choose for cooking it.

Brown rice, which has twice the protein and a much higher count of minerals and vitamins, is unquestionably better for you. It takes a lot longer to cook and is not always suitable for use in all recipes. To serve it plain, it is best steamed. First, wash carefully but do not soak it, then put in a heavy saucepan with a tightly fitting lid. Allow a good 2½ cups of water for each cup of rice and a teaspoon of salt. Boil the rice uncovered for 5 minutes, then lower the heat as much as you can and put the lid on. Allow it to steam gently for 45 minutes. Do not peek! After that, turn the heat off altogether and let it finish steaming undisturbed for another 10 minutes. All the water will be absorbed and the rice tender and fluffy without being gluggy.

Most packets of rice have cooking instructions printed on them and, unless a particular recipe states otherwise, it is best to follow these directions. Boiled white rice can have a little lemon juice added to the cooking water to help keep it nice and white. Pour the rice into boiling salt water in a steady stream, stir it occasionally and drain thoroughly after 12–15 minutes. Just like spaghetti, test a grain or two before draining it to make sure it is cooked to your liking. Drain it well and serve immediately. If you cannot serve it right away, cook it for no more than 12 minutes and then spread it out on a shallow biscuit tray. Cover the rice with foil and leave it in a *very* low oven. Kept warm like this it will not overcook. If intending to use boiled rice in a salad, it is best to add oil and vinegar when the rice is drained and still warm.

Asians prefer cooking short grain rice. For Indian recipes, Patna rice is best. In the Middle East, rice is always fried lightly in a little butter or oil before water or stock is added, then boiled very briskly for a few minutes before being covered and placed in the oven. Whichever way you propose to cook your rice, do watch the time. Nothing is quite as unpleasant to eat as overcooked rice!

Rice in the Alicante Manner

Serves 4-6

Paella is probably the most famous rice dish from Spain, but there are many versions from different parts of the country. This is a delicious and uncomplicated version from Alicante.

500 g green prawns
3 cups water
1½ tsp salt
pinch oregano
¼ tsp saffron threads
1 onion, sliced
¼ cup olive oil
1 red capsicum, seeded and sliced
1 green capsicum, seeded and sliced
1 cup long grain rice

Shell prawns and bring heads and shells to the boil in water with salt, oregano and saffron. Strain and measure 2½ cups stock and set aside. Sauté onion in oil, add prawns. When they turn pink, remove prawns with a slotted spoon. Add sliced capsicums to pan and sauté until glazed. Bring stock to the boil. Add rice to fry pan and pour boiling stock over. Cook briskly for 10 minutes. Add prawns and cover tightly with a lid. Keep on the lowest possible heat for 10-15 minutes until all liquid is absorbed.

Risotto Alla Milanese

Serves 4-6

A cheesy rice dish delicious with vegetables.

2 cups rice
1 tsp saffron threads
4 cups cold beef broth or consomme
1 tsp Vegemite
1 cup Parmesan cheese, grated
3-4 tbls butter

Place rice into saucepan with saffron and broth. Add vegemite and bring to the boil. Stir continuously. Reduce heat, cover and simmer for 15-20 minutes. When all liquid is absorbed and rice is tender stir in cheese and butter. Serve immediately.

Indonesian Rice

Serves 4

100 g long grain rice
pinch turmeric
2 tbls oil
50 g fresh peanuts, skinned
1 tsp cummin seeds
1½ tbls dessicated coconut
salt and pepper

Boil rice in salt water with turmeric. Rinse and drain. Heat oil in fry pan, add rice and stir fry for 3 minutes. Add remaining ingredients, stir and fry 3 minutes more.

Vegetable Risotto

Serves 6

250 g green peas
1 kohlrabi
125 g carrots
125 g parsnips
125 g mushrooms
250 g cooked rice
125 g butter
60 g grated Cheddar cheese
8 tbls sour cream
1 tsp salt
½ cup tomato juice

Shell peas and cut vegetables into small cubes. Cook all vegetables separately until barely tender, or steam if preferred. Mix butter with cheese, cream and tomato juice. Add rice, 1 tsp salt and stir in vegetables. Butter a casserole, pile in mixture, cover and bake in a hot oven for 25 minutes.

Rice and Leeks

Serves 4

2 leeks, trimmed, washed and sliced
3 tbls olive oil
1 cup long grain rice
3 tomatoes, peeled and coarsely chopped
1 tsp brown sugar
1 tsp sea salt
twist of freshly ground pepper
1½ cups boiling water
squeeze of lemon juice

Slice leeks into 3 cm sections, crosswise. Heat oil in large fry pan, add leeks and fork through to break layers. Cook, stirring occasionally, for 5 minutes. Add rice and mix through. Fry, stirring occasionally, until rice is opaque. Add tomatoes, sugar, salt and pepper. Add water. Cover and cook gently until all liquid is absorbed and rice tender. Add more water if necessary. Sprinkle with lemon juice to serve.

Wild Rice and Mushroom Casserole

Serves 4

Wild rice is very nutritious. It is rather more expensive than ordinary rice, but it is still not as expensive as meat.

¼ cup finely chopped onion
¼ cup finely chopped mushrooms
2 tbls butter
1 tbls flour
1 cup beef stock
½ tsp salt and grinding of black pepper
2½ cups cooked wild rice
2 tbls blanched slivered almonds

Wash ⅔ cup uncooked wild rice and soak overnight in cold water. Wash and change water several times. To cook stir into 3 cups of boiling water. Cover and boil 5 minutes, drain and wash again. Add rice and salt to 3 cups boiling water, cover and cook until tender: about 20 minutes. Sauté onions and mushrooms in butter for 5 minutes. Blend in flour with a wooden spoon and gradually add stock, stirring constantly, until smooth and thick. Season to taste and mix with cooked rice. Turn into buttered shallow casserole, sprinkle with almonds and bake in a moderate oven for 20 minutes.

Wild Rice Ring

Serves 4

1 bunch celery, pulped in food
processor
½ cup grated onion
1 cup wild rice
¾ cup pecan nuts
2 tbls parsley, finely chopped
2 tbls basil, finely chopped
1 tbls flour
3 eggs, lightly beaten
1½ cups milk
3 tbls butter, melted
1 tsp salt
freshly ground pepper
4 pecan nuts for decoration

Using steel blade in processor, pulp celery. Remove and squeeze out excess moisture with a tea towel. Grate onion in processor. Place celery and onion into a bowl with rice, nuts, parsley, dill and flour. Stir in eggs, melted butter and milk. Butter a ring mould and fill with mixture. Place mould into a baking dish with enough water to come half way up ring mould. Bake in a moderate oven for 45 minutes. Remove and allow to stand 10 minutes before unmoulding onto a serving plate. Decorate with nuts and serve with fresh tomato sauce (recipe p. 94).

Stuffed Green Peppers

Serves 3-6

Sauce:
450 g tomatoes, skinned and
chopped
60 g butter
1 tbls flour
pinch salt
1 tbls sugar
6 large green peppers
125 g uncooked rice
1 tbls finely chopped parsley
60 g carrots
60 g parsnips
60 g celeriac
60 g shelled peas
60 g butter
1 tbls salt

Prepare sauce first by cooking tomatoes in heavy saucepan over medium heat until tender. In a separate saucepan heat 60 g butter, add flour and make a roux. Take away from heat and strain tomatoes through a sieve into the roux. Return to heat, stirring constantly, add salt, sugar and, when sauce is thick, set aside. Prepare vegetables. Heat butter in a saucepan and stir in rice. When grains become opaque, add chopped vegetables, peas, parsley, salt and stir. Add enough water to reach 2 cm above rice. Cover and simmer 20 minutes undisturbed. Core peppers, stuff with rice mixture and place into shallow casserole. Pour tomato sauce over, cover with foil and bake in a moderate oven for 45 minutes.

Middle Eastern Pilaff

Serves 4

4 tbls oil
2 large onions, chopped
3 stalks celery, chopped into small pieces
2 cloves garlic, crushed
½ cup seedless raisins
½ cup currants
¼ cup pistachio nuts, shelled variety, raw
60 g pine nuts
2 cups long grain rice
8 cups boiling water
2 tsp salt
sour cream or natural yoghurt to serve

Heat 2 tbls oil in large fry pan. Sauté onions and celery for 2 minutes. Add garlic, raisins, currants and nuts. Cook, stirring, for 3 minutes. Remove from pan with slotted spoon and reserve. Add remaining oil to same pan. When hot add rice. Stir for a few minutes until rice begins to colour. Pour boiling water over and add salt. Cover pan and cook 8 minutes, forking through occasionally. All the water should be absorbed; if not, cover with a folded tea towel and cook a further 2 minutes. To serve, stir in onion and fruit mixture.

Indian Spiced Rice

Serves 6

1 cup rice
½ cup oil
1 stick cinnamon
8 cloves
4 cardamom seeds
2 medium onions, sliced
4 bay leaves
½ tsp salt
2 cups water
1 chicken stock cube

Soak rice in water to cover for 20 minutes. Heat oil. When oil is beginning to smoke add cinnamon, cloves and cardamom seeds. Stir, cook 2 minutes. Add onions, stir and cook until glazed. Add bay leaves. Wash and drain rice, add to oil, stir until beginning to colour. Add salt and 2 cups water and mix in stock cube. Transfer to ovenproof dish, or cover pan tightly with a lid and bake in a brisk oven for 5 minutes. Lower heat and bake until rice is tender. Roughly 30 minutes.

Prawn and Corn Pilaff

Serves 6

100 g butter
1 onion, chopped
1 red capsicum, seeded and chopped
225 g long grain rice
50 g peas
150 g corn kernels
bouquet garni
salt and freshly ground pepper
550 ml water
900 g prawns, peeled
25 g seasoned flour

Preheat oven to 190°C. Heat half the butter in a casserole and sauté onion and capsicum 2 minutes. Add rice and stir 1 minute. Add peas, corn, bouquet garni, seasoning and water. Bring to the boil, cover casserole and place in moderate oven for 20 minutes. Dip prawns in flour. Heat remaining butter in a pan and gently fry prawns. Place prawns over rice to serve.

SAUCES, PUREES AND DRESSINGS

In today's kitchen the true and natural taste of vegetables is finally appreciated. Rich and overpowering sauces are a thing of the past, as are the hours once spent in preparing them. The strainer, the sieve, and even the mouli are all being replaced with the quicker and more sophisticated talents of the blender or food processor.

Although there are times when a sauce, such as a béchamel or velouté, based on a roux made of butter and flour, is still used, more often than not today you will find yourself eating a sauce which is a simple purée made from raw or lightly cooked vegetables. Such a sauce can be used to mask another vegetable, as a filling for an omelette, or passed around separately in a sauce boat. Its appearance and taste can be quite sensational.

One word about the preparation of sauces. If you are making one based on a roux, melt your butter over medium heat, stir in the flour and, just as soon as it's blended, remove from the heat and stir in *warmed* stock, milk, cream or vegetable purée. This will prevent lumps forming. When it is thoroughly blended, return to the heat and allow the flour to cook, stirring constantly. If your sauce still goes lumpy, remove from the heat and add more warmed liquid and repeat the process. Or, if you do have a blender or food processor, tip the sauce into the machine and let the machine take out all the lumps! If your sauce is to be thickened with eggs instead of flour, add a little hot sauce to the beaten egg before blending the egg in. Once the egg has been added, never let it boil or it will curdle.

Velouté Sauce

Serves 6-8

When stock is added to a roux of melted butter and flour it is called a velouté sauce; it is the base for any white sauce. The addition of finely chopped mushrooms gives it a different flavour, or the sauce can have 2 tbls of cream added. When béchamel sauce is required, add a liaison of egg yolk and cream, or simply cream. For a less rich sauce, simply add milk to the roux.

2 tbls butter
2 tbls flour
1½ cups stock
salt and pepper

Melt butter, stir in flour with a wooden spoon. Stir over heat 1-2 minutes, remove from heat and gradually stir in stock. Once absorbed return to heat and bring to the boil stirring constantly.

Allow to simmer 5 minutes before using or making other additions.

Sabayon Mousseline Sauce

Makes 1½ cups

This delicious sauce goes well with all vegetables, fish or chicken. Finely chopped herbs may be added or, to make a more piquant sauce, half the stock can be replaced with wine or wine vinegar.

3 egg yolks
½ cup cream
¼ cup chicken stock
90-185 g butter, at room temperature
salt and pepper

All ingredients must be at room temperature. Using steel bowl and wire whisk, stir egg yolks, cream and stock over hot water until sauce coats wire of whisk. Keep moving bowl off and onto heat while whisking and do not allow to overheat. Cut butter into small pieces and whisk in off the heat. If using a food processor, butter should be melted first, the egg mixture placed into processor bowl, and then melted butter poured through the funnel while machine is operating.

Spinach and Pear Purée

Serves 4

Excellent with chicken or fish.

1 large pear, peeled and cored
400 g fresh spinach, stalks removed
30 g butter
salt, pepper and nutmeg

Poach prepared pear for 10-15 minutes covered with water. When tender, drain and set aside to keep warm. Wash spinach and tear into small pieces. Cook 2-3 minutes with only the water from washing clinging to it. Place spinach and pear into blender or food processor and purée.

Watercress Purée

Serves 4

1 bunch watercress
lemon juice
1-2 tbls cream

Remove coarse stalks of watercress and place into large saucepan of boiling salt water for 2-3 minutes. Drain, refresh under cold water in colander. Purée in blender or food processor with metal blade. Add a little lemon juice and cream through funnel until desired consistency. Use immediately.

Pea Purée

Serves 6

375 g shelled peas
3-4 spring onions, peeled
1 tsp sugar
1 tsp salt
sprig fresh mint
fresh cream

Cook peas and onions with sugar, salt and mint in water to cover for 5 minutes. Drain and place in blender or food processor to purée, adding cream for desired consistency.

Cooked Tomato Sauce

Makes 2 cups

Can be stored in refrigerator in a sealed jar for a few days.

¼ cup olive oil
1 large onion, chopped
1 clove garlic, chopped
½ cup parsley, finely chopped
1 k tomatoes, peeled and chopped
1 tbls sugar
salt to taste

Heat oil and fry onion, garlic and parsley over low heat until very soft. Add tomatoes, sugar and salt. Cool for 45 minutes stirring occasionally. Cook slightly and purée in blender or processor.

Fresh Tomato Sauce

Makes 2 cups

This sauce will keep for 24 hours in the refrigerator.

1 large onion
1 k tomatoes, peeled and chopped
1 tbls basil, finely chopped
1 tbls sugar
salt to taste

Grate onion in food processor. Change to metal blade and add roughly chopped tomatoes, basil, sugar and salt. Purée for a few seconds. This may need to be done in 2 batches, depending on the size of your processor bowl.

Spanish Green Sauce

To be served with vegetables or fish.

¼ cup olive oil
2 cloves garlic
½ cup parsley, finely chopped
2 tbls flour
½ tsp salt
¼ tsp powdered ginger
freshly ground white pepper
½ cup water
½ cup dry white wine
2 tbls cream

Heat oil in fry pan, sauté garlic until golden then remove. Add garlic to parsley in a bowl and mash well. Add next 4 ingredients, blend well and return to fry pan over moderate heat. Stir constantly and slowly add water, wine and cream.

Maltese Orange Sauce

Serves 4

This is a taste sensation when served with asparagus, artichokes, broccoli or cauliflower. The Maltese orange is a blood orange not always available here, so when making this sauce with ordinary oranges, it is essential to add a drop or two of cochineal — too little rather than too much!

2 blood oranges
2 egg yolks, lightly whisked
90 g butter

Take fine parings from the rind of one of the oranges with a potato peeler. Squeeze out the juice of the same orange and set aside. Grate the rind of the other orange and cut its flesh into small dice, discarding all pith. Melt butter in a double boiler, add grated rind and then, drop by drop, the juice. Whisk gently all the time. Reduce heat so that water is barely boiling. Add yolks and continue to whisk while sauce thickens and doubles in volume. Add diced orange flesh and cook, whisking, 2 minutes more. Add cochineal now if necessary. Before serving the sauce sprinkle the strips of rind into sauce.

Skordalia

This is a traditional Greek dressing which enhances new potatoes, cauliflower, carrots and beans. It is equally good used as a dressing for avocado or a salad, and will keep for a few days in the refrigerator. If it has been stored there, allow it to return to room temperature before using.

2 cloves garlic, crushed
2 tsps salt
60 g freshly ground almonds
2 tbls lemon juice
8 tbls olive oil

Place the first 4 ingredients into your blender and give them a quick whizz. Gradually add the olive oil as if you were making mayonnaise. If you have no machine, crush the garlic with salt and gradually work in remaining ingredients.

Index